Bait Man
Down the Road

Tales of a Tennessee Bait Dealer

About

Friends, Places, And Things

By
Floyd Poindexter

Best Wishes Margaret Ann

Floyd Poindexter

Bait Man

Down the Road...

ISBN 0-9677681-0-1

Published by Stroud Graphics Inc.
1865 Airlane Dr. #12
Nashville, Tenn. 37210
(615) 885-8332

Printed by Rich Printing Co.
3171 centenial Blvd.
Nashville, Tenn. 37209
(615) 350-8747

ACKNOWLEDGMENTS

Friends are the most important part of any persons life and being. To the many friends I have known who have been a part of these tales, I owe a special thanks. To those who have shared a moment of laughter or provided a thought for these tales, a "thank you" seems so much in order.

To my wife, Betty, and my family, thanks for sharing in these stories as they were being put together.

A very special thanks to my beloved niece, Beth, who had the idea to put these tales together. Her encouragement and insistence made it all happen. Thanks Beth. Thanks to everyone who had a part.

Floyd Poindexter, 1999

DEDICATION

This book is dedicated to my father, who started the business in 1965. Also to my mother who was a tremendous help to him in the early years of starting the business. It is dedicated to the many customers we have had through the years and to all who have helped to make my job truly a pleasure, this is for you.

My beloved niece, Beth

INTRODUCTION

Having worked over twenty years as a wholesale bait dealer, I have come in contact with some interesting and wonderful people. Soon after my niece, Beth, graduated from college, she finally got the time to go with me on a route. It was a fun day and one I had anticipated for a long time.

I started to think of all the shops and stores we would be calling on that day and all the people I wanted her to meet. As we rode over the route, stories of people, places and things kept coming to mind. Some of the things were funny, some were ridiculous and some were truly sad.

At the end of the day she had made every step of a long, hard, tiring day with me. It had been great fun for me. We had met some interesting people, we saw some beautiful sites, encountered a family of deer, had a good lunch and really had a good time.

As we worked along, Beth was fascinated by the people, the different stores and shops and some of the tales

which I told of times gone by. As we neared home at the end of the day, Beth said, "You should write a book about all the things you have seen during these years." I just laughed it off and said "No books." As the days and weeks passed, Beth continued her encouragement. She said "You really should write it all down."

After considering Beth's request for several weeks, I decided I would at least make an effort, however feeble it might be to tell some of these tales to you as I told them to her.

All the stories are true as clearly as I can recall with many names being changed to protect the guilty. It is not my intent to denigrate or belittle anyone in any way. All is intended in good fun.

CONTENTS

THE BAIT DEALER

I'm up each morning before the dawn,
To load my truck with bait.
To all my customers I will go,
Those fishermen just can't wait.

With all my tanks and boxes filled,
My truck has quite a load.
I'll check it once, I'll check it twice,
And then I'll hit the road.

Along the way I'll make my stops,
To see what I can sell.
And even on the busiest days,
A story I might tell.

About those fish that did not bite,
Or the one that got away.
I'll work and drive and talk and laugh,
That's how I make my day.

And as I go from store to store,
And many friends have found.
I'll wind up with an empty truck.
So then I'm homeward bound.

My wife, Betty, catching Blue Gill

GETTING STARTED

I started in the bait business with my daddy in 1974. He had started the business several years before and had built it into a retail and wholesale bait business before he retired in 1976.

When I entered the business our plan was for me to start with the wholesale business and he was to work the retail. We planned to help each other.

Of course the first order of business was for me to meet all the customers out on the road and learn the routes. I remember well. This was going to be different from anything I had ever done and was somewhat scary. We had a new truck daddy had just bought and it was rigged as well as it could be to do the job we had to do. He planned to go with me on each route about twice or as many times as it took to meet every customer.

As we started out on the route I soon learned that each stop was as different as day and night. The physical size of some of the large commercial docks and tackle shops was intimidating. I soon learned the people were mostly good, honest, hard working people who had a job to do and were more than willing to help me in doing my job.

RED'S BAIT HOUSE

Daddy went with me on the first day. I drove and he pointed the way. I sensed early on there were stops that were strictly business and there were some that were fun. One of his favorite stops was Red's Bait House. This was a man and woman who sold bait from their basement. "Red" had acquired his nick-name from his ruddy complexion in his younger years. Daddy affectionately called them "Mr. Red" and "Mrs. Red." They had sold bait all their lives. Mr. and Mrs. Red were well past retirement age when I first met them. Mrs. Red was a grand-motherly lady with a warm smile. She was a joy to all who knew her.

Before we could get their bait from the truck and into the basement Mrs. Red called down from the back steps

"I want y'all to come up and try some of my peach pie 'fore you go." Mrs. Red always had something she wanted you to "try."

She would say "Come up and try my soup" or "come try some of my corn bread and beans."

As we continued on the route I made maps and notes which helped me remember names when I went back the next week. This seemed kind of like cheating but it works. It's real bad when you go back next trip and say "Hello Bill" and the guy's name is Murf.

U.L.

On down the road, daddy said, "This next stop you may want to skip. You can stop if you like." I didn't understand right off because daddy always liked most everybody and if he didn't you could just about bet he had a reason. I asked "What's the deal?" He said "There's this big overgrown, smart ass boy there and I don't like to hear him."

I could hardly wait to stop. As we

got out of the truck and started toward the shop the front door flew open and out came U.L. Before daddy could say "Meet my son, Floyd" U.L. said in a loud, laughing voice, "Hey old man, what kind of trash are you peddling today?" Daddy turned around and got back in the truck.

I sold U.L. a lot of bait over the next two years till he sold his shop. We are good friends to this day. You just have to know how to handle him.

OLD MAN SELBY

On up the road a few miles daddy told me to pull over at a small roadside park. Not knowing why he wanted to stop, I pulled in and stayed in the truck. He jumped out and went to the back of the truck. He then came to the front of the truck and set six boxes of night crawlers in the seat between us. Back then we sold bulk night crawlers in boxes containing about a gallon of dirt and a gallon of night crawlers. Not knowing what was going on, again I asked, "What's the deal?" He said "Down the road there's an old man who likes to break open every box on the truck, dig around in all of them, and then buy one box. He said "I always hide all but one box before I get to him."

I thought this seemed a little strange so I had to see for myself. A couple of weeks later when I started running by myself I left all the boxes in the back of the truck. Guess what! Sure enough, he busted them all open and scattered worms and dirt all over the truck.

Now old man Selby was a rare bird but he was good for a few laughs over the years. You just had to hide all your extra worms from him.

One day I pulled into his parking lot and he was asleep in the back of his small bait shop. It was about mid-morning. As I bounded from the truck to enter the front door he looked at me with utter disgust, mumbled some four and six letter words and said "I thought I was about to have my first customer of the day!"

It took quite a while to get to know old man Selby. Up until I got to know him he would ruin an otherwise good day. I even tried to run the route backwards and run him toward the end of the day so I wouldn't have as much day left for him to ruin.

I remember he would always quiz me about the condition and size of the minnows I was hauling. Regardless of weather, how good or how bad fishing was, and regardless of how many he might need, he would always buy just two pounds.

On a typical day he would ask, "What you haulin' boy?" Crappie minnows Mr. Selby. "How long you had 'em on hand?" Got 'em yesterday. "Are they in good shape?" They are in real good shape Mr. Selby. "They got a lotta kick to 'em?" Yeah they kickin' real good Mr. Selby. "Good, I'll take two pounds."

One day I was feeling good and having a good day. I pulled into his lot. He came running to the truck and said "What you haulin' boy?" I said "Crappie minnows Mr. Selby. I had 'em on hand about six months. They've got the bug eyes, the red gill and they're eat up with the fungus. They're all weak, a lot of 'em are dying and what ain't dying have got the spins! How many do you want?" He said "Gimme two pounds."

Old Man Selby

GREEN'S BAIT SHOP

Another of daddy's favorite stops was Green's Bait Shop. The Greens sold bait from the basement of their house. Mr. and Mrs. Green were lovely people, pleasant to deal with and were always a joy. It always amazed me at the amount of bait these people sold and the only advertisement they had was a small sign at the entrance to their driveway that read "FISH BAIT".

After many years of selling they took down their sign and retired. They both had some health problems and had gotten tired. Through the summer and fall I had been busy and soon it was Christmas and I had not seen Mr. and Mrs. Green in several months. The day before Christmas I drove up to visit them for a while. As I walked from their driveway across the yard they both came out on the front porch, clapping their hands and laughing and crying and saying "We knew you'd come back, We knew you'd come back." I couldn't have had a better Christmas.

MR. AND MRS. LACK

Many of the people I met on those first runs have retired and many have passed on. One of those that has passed on was an interesting old fellow who made his living selling fish bait, digging ginseng, repairing clocks, guns and lawn mowers. He was innovative and could repair almost anything. If he needed a special tool to do a job he would make the tool and then do the job. He had a dry wit and an odd sense of humor. If I could work a smile out of him I knew I had done good. His wife was a lovely lady who smiled all the time.

One day I entered their bait shop and she was emptying the minnow tank. She was dipping the water with a big bucket and dashing it out a nearby window. Only about half of the water was hitting the window. I stood there in amazement. Water was going everywhere. She continued until she must have sensed that someone was watching. She turned around and smiled and said

Down on the Creek

"I just love to play in water."

They lived on a state highway with a small creek running just behind their house. For many years they had an outdoor toilet mounted on the edge of the creek. The front of the toilet was set on the edge of the creek bank with a cable on each front corner anchored to a tree up in the yard. It was a sight to see, complete with a moon on the door and the whole nine yards. I have regretted I never got a picture of it.

MR. MYERS

Several of the smaller shops were run by people who sold bait from their basements or garages. One in particular I remember was a small little hump shouldered man who sold minnows from a wire basket sunk in a spring-fed branch behind his house. He took great pride in the number of years he had sold minnows. I sold him minnows for several years. Each trip I had to walk across a long pole that had been placed across the branch where he kept his minnow box. The pole had been hewn flat on top and served as a cross walk across the branch which was several feet below. Through the years I kept thinking the pole would break as I crossed. It never did.

One day when I stopped he came from his porch and met me at the branch. He said "I got something I want to tell you boy. I been here a long time and you've been the best bait dealer I ever had. I've got to quit selling 'cause my spring has gone dry and time has took it's toll on me." He said "I guess me and the spring played out at about the same time."

I thanked him for everything and especially for being so good to me over the years. I turned to go back to my truck. As I walked away he said "Hey boy." I stopped and turned back to look at him as he stood there in his humped over, near fetal stance. He smiled and said "Honey, I wish you well." I cried as I drove on down the road to my next stop.

LEARNING ROUTES AND OTHER THINGS

Being in the bait business was so totally different from what I had always done. I had worked in the printing business from the first day I graduated from high school. Strangely it turned out I worked in the printing business twenty years to the day. Even though daddy only lived about three years after I got into the bait business he taught me a lot. He taught me never to take a friend or a customer for granted. He always had taught me to do the very best job I could do. He never counted his chickens before they hatched. He believed in working hard and doing your best.

In showing me the routes he explained that he usually tried to run a circle or a loop that would not entail a lot of backtracking. He explained that if I had a preference for running these loops and I wanted to change it would be fine. Immediately I decided the big route he had run clockwise, I would much prefer to run counter clockwise, after all I was somewhat in charge now. At the end of a long day I got to the last customer, which had previously been the first customer. Early in the day this customer had sensed the truck was late and they had called the shop to see where I was. Not knowing I was running backwards they assured the customer I was on my way. Now picture this. As I walked into the bait room of one of the best customers we had, there stood this lady looking a hole through me. "Where have you been?" she demanded. I said "I've been running my route." She asked "All day?" "I called early this morning and they said you were on your way!"

Now I had never met this lady but I well knew I was in big trouble. She continued to lecture while pacing back and forth like a drill instructor. "I have had customers waiting all day for bait!" "This is the first pretty day we have had in weeks and us with no bait!" "All day we wait for you and you get here at dark!"

She looked straight at me and said, "Now that you are here, go to your truck and bring us one hundred cups of night crawlers and twenty pounds of minnows." I swallowed a couple of times and said "I don't have any." She came unglued! She said "If all you have is an empty truck, why did you even bother to stop?" I said "I just wanted to see how much you wanted if I had any." "I'll go get what you need and I'll be back in three hours." She said "That's not soon enough!" I got on the phone and called daddy. I needed help. He said "Wait right there, I'll be there with what you need in one hour and fifteen minutes." He made it.

To this day I admire and respect this lady immensely. She is a good friend and treasured customer.

THE FIREMAN

I knew a man who built a market and bait shop into a good business while working a full time job as a fireman. He and his wife had worked hard for a long time building the business and adding inventory. As he neared retirement age the store and the business became too much for them. Because of his age, his insurance and retirement with the fire department he decided to keep his job as a fireman and sell the store.

Two young guys bought the store. In the days to come while servicing the account I asked the new owners how they liked the store business. "Didn't know it could be so good." was the reply. They said if they had known they could have had incomes like that they would have had a store a long time ago. Within a few weeks the inventory had been converted to two new cars, two new trucks and a boat, the store closed.

SIGNS ALONG THE WAY

I have often wondered if other people enjoy reading signs along the road as I do. Now I don't mean to make fun but some of the stuff I have seen is really funny. Besides checking all the backward and upside down letters I like to check for spelling. I get to laugh at myself quite often when my wife points out some of my misteaks.

I once saw a sign on an adding machine that said, "ADDER FORY SAIL." The next trip when I went back it was gone so it must have "sailed." Then there was the yard sale sign way out in the country that advertised "FREE PARKING." I saw a large sheet of plywood nailed over the front door of a service station that was spray painted "WE'RE CLOSED Y'ALL." Not long ago I saw an expensive sign that read "HAIR WE ARE."

By far the most interesting sign of all was one I saw about ten years ago. I had watched this homestead grow over a seven or eight year period. It started as a small trailer set up beside a lot where several dumpsters were set. The dumpsters and the trailer were well back off the highway. It has continually grown over the years. The trailer has lean-tos, add-ons, extensions, dog houses, chicken coops, junk cars and the biggest conglomeration of junk that you can imagine. There were piles of used lumber and sheet metal, refrigerators, stoves, car tires and worn out furniture. You name it, they had it all.

We all have seen large banners or signs stretched across city streets that advertise various events such as county fairs or car races. These people had gotten one of these signs and stretched it across the front of their trailer. It read "WELCOME SPORTS FANS."

WATERMELON BOY

I am reminded of a little boy over in Jackson County who was selling watermelons. I saw his sign and stopped to see what he had. It was hot and he had sweat and dirt running down his face. He looked to be about ten years old. I said "I'll take the one on the end." He said "They're $1.25 each, you take two and I'll let you have them for $1.00 each." I said "Give me the two on the end." He loaded them as quick as a flash. I said, "I wonder if I might pay you when my horse wins a race?" "No sir! It'll be $2.00 now 'cause your horse might not ever win a race". I flipped him $2.00 and started to my truck thinking about how sharp he was. Before I could start my truck he looked up at me with a big smile and said "I'll tell you something else, you might not even have a horse."

LIZARD BOYS

A year or two later I was over in the same area and I saw two boys hot footin' down the road with minnow buckets in their hands. I stopped to give them a ride. As we rode they figured out from the tanks on the truck I was a bait dealer. The older boy who was about twelve years old, said, "We got spring lizards, how about you buying some." Then he said "We'll get off down at the big cross-road."

When we got to the cross road I got out to negotiate the deal. It was quite clear, the older boy was the businessman. The younger was into music. He was whipping out a pretty good rhythm on his arm harp. He was not a Johann Sebastian Bach or a Wolfgang Mozart, but he was good. The boy had potential. The older boy said, "We get $1.50 a dozen but if you take 'em all they're $1.25.

I don't normally sell lizards because you can't begin to buy as many as you could sell. They are not raised commercially so the only ones you can get are caught in the wild.

I agreed to take them all so they dumped them all into one bucket and started counting back into the empty bucket. I knew they didn't want to part with their bucket so I went to the front of the truck to get something to put them in. The only thing I could find was a styrofoam chest where I had some drinks. I emptied the chest and went back to the back of the truck with it. "We got 21 dozen but we're throwing in the odd dozen for good measure. We put in plenty of moss so they won't get hot." I paid them $25.00 and down the road I went.

About thirty miles down the road

a little light went on in my head. When I got home I counted the lizards, all twelve dozen of them and lots of moss.

MY FRIEND DAVID

I once had a customer named David who had just opened a bait shop. One day I walked into his shop and the first thing he said was "You got any lizards?" I told him I never sold them and explained how you could never get them when you needed them.

He said "I sold one man sixty dozen yesterday at $5.00 a dozen." He's coming back this weekend and he'll take all I can get." As I started to leave David reminded me again, "If you run into any lizards I'll pay $3.00 a dozen for all you can get."

About thirty miles down the road I sold night crawlers to an old gal I called "Dirty Mouth Pam." While I was in her store a kind of shy acting man walked in and set a big box on the floor. Pam asked him "What can I do for you?" He quietly and shyly said, "I got lizards and I was thinking maybe you might like to buy some." Old Pam went off. "Get you and your lizards to hell out of my store NOW!

I followed him out and I asked,"How many lizards do you have?" He said "About 125 dozen. They're good lizards but I ain't having much luck selling them." I asked "How much are they?" He said "$1.25 a dozen." I took them all. He was as straight as an arrow. He insisted I watch as he counted.

I backtracked back to David's, made out his bill and set the lizards on the floor. He couldn't believe his eyes. We both had a good day.

David had started his bait shop in an old building that had been vacant for several years. He remodeled, patched and painted and opened for business in the spring. I got to know David and enjoyed talking with him right off. He was always asking advice which I tried to give when I could. He was a young handsome guy with a beautiful wife. He had worked in a big grocery store for about twelve years before going into business for himself. He worked hard and his business grew. Over a period of time he added a fruit stand, which did well, and gas pumps were added. He was over the hump, he was on his way. Occasionally he showed me his books. I really didn't care to see because I don't even look at my own, but his figures were impressive. He was doing good.

Over a five or six month period I noticed he had become withdrawn. He lost a lot of weight and never had much to say. One day I asked "David, are you on a diet?" He said "Yeah, I lost about thirty pounds." Then trying to joke it off he said "The 130 pounds I lost last summer is what really got me. My wife left me and I'll be closing the store soon." The building stands vacant to this day.

Time passes and things change. As I drive along I can't help but remember a lot of people and times gone by. Some are funny and some are sad.

BROWN EXPLOSION

One day up in the country I fell in behind an old car. It was clunking along about forty. The fenders were hanging loose kind of like the wings on a settin' hen. In the back seat was a little boy and up front, driving was this big, big guy that I guessed to be the little boy's grandfather. Now, when we were kids, we've all hung out the window of a car and played airplane with our hands cutting through the air back and forth and up and down. It was fun. That's what this kid was doing.

The big guy driving was chewing tobacco. All of a sudden he decided to spit out the window. It looked like a brown explosion coming out the side of the car. The little boy caught it right in the face. He started wiping his face and was doing some kind of acrobatics in the back seat of the car. The old man drove on like nothing had happened. It doesn't take much to amuse a bait dealer.

Brown Explosion

"RED" and "YARD DOG"

Some of the people I had the good fortune to deal with in the past have been older people who have retired from another career or job. One of these was a man I only knew as "Red." "Red" was an easy going, likable guy who always seemed to have a big smile. He worked for two of the big commercial docks where I sold bait. He worked as a dock hand, pumping gas, selling bait, and moving boats around and doing small repairs around the dock.

"Red" had worked a long and colorful career in law enforcement before he decided to slow his pace and work as a dock hand. He worked a lengthy time as a highway patrolman, then as chief of police in two small towns. He always liked telling or hearing a good tale and he liked to fish.

He said back when he was much younger, he fished a lot of trot lines and limb lines. One day he had worked his way up the lake hanging limb lines. He said it was getting on up in the day and he had put out several lines and was quite a distance up the lake. He said as he came up on a boat dock he knew his breakfast was wearing thin. He said the smell of food cooking, wafting out across the cove, reminded him of that fact even more. He said he went on to the dock, thinking maybe he could get some coffee or maybe even some lunch. He said the boy doing the cooking poured him a cup of coffee. As he drank the coffee the boy said, "If you can wait till it's done, we would like for you to stay and eat with us." "Red" said, "It smells mighty good, what are you cooking?" "Hawk

Hawk and Dumplings

and dumplings" was the reply. "Red" said, "I don't think I ever ate any hawk and dumplings, what's it like?" The boy replied, "It's a lot like owl and dumplings except it ain't as tough." "Red" declined.

"Red" worked at one of the docks with a guy named "Yard Dog." "Yard" was a likable guy who liked to have a good time. The word around the dock was he really did like a good party.

"Red" said one day "Yard" invited him to a party he was having that night down by the lake. He thought about it a minute and then asked who else had been invited. "Yard" called off a few names. "Red" said most of the people he named, he remembered from his law enforcement days. He told "Yard" he didn't think he would be able to attend because his bullet proof vest was at the cleaners and he didn't think he could get a military escort on that short notice.

"Yard" thought about his guest the rest of the afternoon and then decided he wouldn't even go to his own party.

ROGER

My friend, Roger worked for one of the commercial docks which I serviced a few years back. Roger was a dock hand and fishing guide. He was a likable guy who liked a good joke and was always having fun.

Working for the boat dock gave him the opportunity to meet a lot of vacationing fishermen who were anxious to learn how and where to catch a lot of big bass. Roger always knew how and where. He also knew that if he did his job too well, his services as a guide would be a one shot deal. The lake where he worked and fished was a clear-water lake, full of good smallmouth and largemouth bass, which made for excellent night fishing.

Roger knew, any fisherman who was worth his salt could catch on to how he fished but he had a plan that kept them from learning his favorite banks. Even though his favorite banks were just across the lake from the dock where he worked, he would take them down the lake to the big water and make a big circle and a figure eight and then back up the lake to where they had just been. You can easily get lost on this lake with it's high hills and deep hollows, even in the daytime.

After fishing most of the night, Roger would make the same run down the lake and back again before returning to the dock. He would laugh about them catching most of their fish in sight of the dock, and never knowing where they had been.

One day while I was putting in bait at the dock, Roger started to bug me about how much money I was making selling them bait. While I was stocking them for a big weekend he continued to bug me. After I had finished and started to make out their bill, he leaned over where he could see my ticket book as I wrote. I ignored him and acted like I didn't see him. I flipped open the ticket book, wrote the name of the dock and the date at the top. I knew they had gotten crickets, minnows, and night crawlers, so I quickly added the three items in my head, counted down three spaces and filled in the total. Then I went back and filled in the three items as Roger shook his head and walked away.

Each trip I made after that day, Roger always got where he could see my ticket book as I made out their bill. Each time I acted like I didn't see him. Always, I would count down the correct number of spaces, draw a line and fill in the total first. Roger would always shake his head and walk away. When I was going to have a ticket that had several odd items with odd amounts that were clearly more than I could add in my head, I would run the total on my pocket calculator while I was at the truck and write it down in the palm of my hand. After getting back to the dock, I would open my ticket book, draw a line and fill in the total while Roger looked on.

It worked on his mind so much, each time there was a new dock hand, Roger would whisper to him and then they would both watch as I filled in the total first. It was fun.

One day Roger quit his job at the dock and started driving a truck. About ten years later, I came in from a route and my son, Buddy, said, "There was a truck driver here to see you today, who worked at a boat dock where you sold bait." "He said something about how you always made out a bill, starting with the total and worked your way up." I knew it had to be Roger.

BAD CUP OF WORMS

I sold bait some time ago to a lady who bought an old store and cleaned it up and built it into a good business. Occasionally this lady's mother ran the store for her. Her mother was witty and had a good sense of humor.

One day I went into the store when the mother was there. As I entered she said, "I have a question." She said, "A man came here yesterday and said he had bought a cup of worms here and baited his hook one time and the rest of the worms were dead." She said,

"I think he was fibbing, but what should I have done?" I said, "Give him another cup of worms or give his money back or sing him a song or whatever it takes to make him happy." I went on to explain that sometimes fishermen go down to the lake and the sun is hot, it cooks their bait, it blisters the hide off them, the mosquitoes and chiggers eat them up pretty good and they don't catch any fish. I said "They want somebody to jump off on and it just happened to be you."

She looked at me and said "You make fishing sound like it's not just a lot of fun."

Quickly I said, "Oh, no, I didn't mean it that way. The ones that go and keep their bait cool and lively, catch a lot of fish and stay out of the way of the chiggers and mosquitoes have a lot of fun, they just don't come back and tell you about it."

She gave me a big smile. She was always such a joy.

DIVINE INTERVENTION

I had a customer named Darryl who ran a small country store. In his store he sold snacks, groceries and drinks. At lunch time he served pizzas, barbecue sandwiches and fried chicken. I always seemed to get to his store around lunch time. I enjoyed talking to Darryl and lunch was always good. I was always amazed at the signs around his store which were usually done by hand with a magic marker. Along with the signs showing prices of everything, there were signs with bible verses. They were on the front door and throughout the store. You just got the feeling Darryl was a good and righteous man.

One day while in his store we got to discussing bait sales in general, which were in a slump at the time. I suggested that it might be the terribly hot weather we were having. He said his small son had gone fishing one day with his grandpa. He said it was one of those days when it was really hot and the fish were not biting.

He said the little guy had watched his grandpa fish all morning and had not had a bite. He really did want to see grandpa catch a fish.

Now, Darryl had always taught the little boy to live in a Godly and righteous way. He had taught him to say his prayers and just to do what was right. As the little boy watched grandpa fish and the day wore on and the sun got hotter, he thought maybe some divine intervention was what grandpa needed. He remembered the admonition, "Pray without ceasing." I. Thessalonians 5:17. He remembered "Ask, and it shall be given you; seek, and ye shall find." Matthew 7:7. He decided a prayer might help and he knew certainly it would not hurt. The little boy began to pray. "Oh God, would you help grandpa to catch a fish." "And oh God, maybe you could let it be about the biggest fish in this lake!" The little boy had not much more than said "Amen," when he looked up and grandpa was getting a bite. His rod had bent over and was about to be jerked from the boat. Grandpa cranked on the reel as he followed the big fish from one end of the boat to the other. Back and forth he went as his line cut through the water. The battle was on. Finally after several minutes the big fish wore down and grandpa lifted it into the boat. Now, grandpa was disappointed because the big fish was really big, but it was a carp. The little boy, not knowing one fish from the other was elated. He was as excited as he had ever been. His little heart was pounding. He said "Grandpa, you did it, you did it."

After the excitement wore down the little boy said. "Grandpa, you did good, but I need to tell you, we got to give God credit for that fish." He said, "I was praying for that fish just seconds before you caught it."

Grandpa said, "That's fine son, but next time you speak to Him, make sure you mention "Walleye."

SMOKED ALMONDS

One day on this same road I stopped to sell a customer some bait. As I collected for the bait I noticed a rack of smoked almonds on the check-out counter. Everybody puts all the good stuff on the check-out counter. I bought a big bag as I left. On down the road a short distance I noticed I needed some gas. I pulled into a station and started to pump the gas. I then reached back into the truck and got the bag of smoked almonds and opened them. As I turned around I noticed this woman had joined me at the pumps. She was watching me pretty good so I checked the pump to see if it was self service. It was. She continued looking at me.

I asked "Would you like to have some smoked almonds?" She said "I don't mind if I do." I handed her the bag and she took some and handed me the bag back. I laid it on the side of the truck and topped off my tank and hung up the nozzle. She was still looking at me. I said "You like to have some more almonds?" She said "You know I believe I will." I paid her for the gas and she handed me the bag. It had one almond in it. Now nobody in his right mind would mess up his lips for one smoked almond.

FRESH CORN

One of the things I have enjoyed over the years is the opportunity to stop along the road and buy vegetables or stop at garage sales or yard sales. Even though my schedules have been tight I have stopped hundreds of times and met lots of people. Most all have been the absolute salt of the earth.

I stopped a few years back to buy some corn. Two ladies were selling from a small wagon at the side of a farm house. The lady ahead of me bought six dozen ears and I had ordered six dozen ears. While they were counting and boxing mine, two men came from the corn field back behind the house with a fresh picked load. I quickly

Fresh Corn

decided this was two husband and wife couples who were partners in the corn venture. It was mid-July and it was forever more blazin' hot. Tempers were getting a little short. One of the ladies was a real talker. As soon as the men stopped the tractor she started. "Thought y'all never was gonna get back." "We just about out on this first load." "We been countin' just as fast as we can ever since y'all been gone, we really been working."

The older man looked up over his glasses and said without cracking a smile "Good, that's about what we expected of you!"

OLD ALBERT

Not far on down the road there was a little old man and a big woman who opened a bait shop. Now I know it's not nice to talk about anybody's size

Old Albert

but this was really a mismatch. She was a whopper and he was just plain little. She talked like an auctioneer and he never said anything. About all I ever knew about them was his name was Albert. They just stayed open long enough for the light bill to come due about twice.

When I would enter the store he would be standing there with his hands in his pockets up to his elbows and she would say "Now Albert, we got six cups of night crawlers left from last week, If we get six more we'll have twelve. That'll be enough don't you think Albert? It's looking like rain and fishin' ain't too good, huh Albert?" "Okay give us six cups, cause I think six with the six we already got will be enough." "Right, Albert?" Before Albert could say a word she'd say, "Yeah, go ahead and give us six." I would go to the truck and get six cups. Old Albert hasn't said anything yet.

WOMAN IN THE ROAD

This next sequence of events happened about fifteen years ago. At first I thought I might not even include it because it is quite bizarre to say the least and some of the conditions surrounding it are a bit sad.

Again, I don't intend to denigrate anybody so I'll tell it exactly as I recall with no names included.

One day I had been down a dead end road delivering some bait and was back-tracking out. It was a paved country road. There were mostly pastures and few houses along the road. Up ahead about a quarter mile I noticed a woman walking in the same direction I was going. She was dressed in hot pink shorts and walking in the middle of the road. She was high stepping like a show horse and as I got closer I started to think, "What kind of deal is this?"

As I got even closer she started weaving and collapsed right in the middle of the road. I started to think fast. I didn't know if she was sick and needed help or if it was some kind of trap. I had a younger sister who was a diabetic almost all her life so I knew this lady could be in trouble. I decided I had to stop. I slowly pulled past her and stopped just as she was at the rear of my truck. I left my door open and engine running. I went to the rear of the truck where she lay. Her purse had spilled and there was money and keys all over the road. I clasped both her hands and began to look around. Down in the pasture, about fifty yards away, there was a car parked. I held tightly to her hands and shielded myself from the car as best I could. As she started to wake up I asked her if she was a diabetic or if she had heart problems. She said "No." As I helped her up, still holding her hands, I kept watching the car. I asked "Whose car is that?" She said it was hers. I noticed there was an electric fence along the road as far as I could see. I asked "How did you get the car down in the pasture?" She then nodded toward a house far across the pasture and said "I live back there in that house." As I continued to talk to her I released her hands and helped her gather up her belongings. I had decided it was not a trap. She said "I must have taken too much of my medicine this morning."

I asked if I could call a doctor or a friend or neighbor. She said "No, I'm all right." She asked me to help her across the fence and down to her car, which I did. She got in the car and sat down. She assured me she could drive across the pasture home.

As I started back to my truck she said "There's one more thing I need." Then she started to smile and said, "No, you probably wouldn't want to do that." Then she said "Or maybe you would, I want some sex." I said "You're trying to get us killed!" I asked "Are you married?" She said "Yeah, my old man is fifty going on seventy and I'm forty going on thirty." "He's down the road getting some canes." About that time I looked back up to the road and there set a truck loaded with tobacco stalks. Out jumped two men. She said "That's my husband, don't you tell him anything."

I thought "Oh, Floyd, you have screwed up now." I started to my truck thinking if that electric fence didn't get me, the old farmer would. As I jumped the fence he met me. "Did you hurt my wife?" "No sir." "As I came up the road she collapsed in the road in front of me." He demanded, "Did you run over her?" "NO sir, she's all right, she's down there in the car in the field." I talked to her and she seemed to be all right." I looked back down toward the car and she was walking toward home. She was about half way across a fifty acre field.

He said "I just got her out of the institution and she's done this twice already." I said "I sure hope she gets along all right and if it's all right with you I do need to be going."

BABY IN THE ROAD

Over in another county a few years ago I was driving on another country road and I found a baby. This road is full of curves and humps. I popped up over one of these humps and there stood a little girl in the road. I went past her and stopped. Not wanting to scare her I eased up to her asking "Where's mama?" She said "Mama, mama" but that was all she could say. I guessed her to be less than two years old. She was a little doll. She came to me and I started walking up the road to a house trying to find where she came from. An elderly man and woman came to the door and I asked them if they knew who she belonged to. They didn't so I asked them if they would hold her until I could go back and move my truck out of the road. They did. I parked my truck and then took the baby on up a dead end road where there was a mobile home. The front door was open and the television was blaring. Inside there was a woman I guessed to be the little girl's grandmother. She didn't even know how long the little girl had been gone.

SHADE TREE MECHANIC

I have seen a lot of little mishaps along the road but luckily none I have seen were ever really bad. Mostly what I have had have been minor. I remember one time I had a carriage bearing go out on my truck. A carriage bearing is a rubber mounted bearing that holds the drive shaft. It's not a big job but out on the road with no tools it can be quite a problem. I managed to make it to a country store and asked the store keeper if she knew a mechanic or someone with a tow truck.

Standing back in the corner was a man who overheard what I had asked. He stood and looked at me for a minute and he asked what kind of trouble I had. I told him and he said "I can fix it. You will have to go with me to get my tools and the new bearing first." The lady in the store told me she didn't know him and I was beginning to wonder if I should go with him. He really didn't look like a mechanic but I needed help, I decided to go.

As we rode I asked him where he worked. He said he was laid off right then. We rode on. I asked him where he lived. He said "Out the ridge." He didn't talk much. I never could get him into a conversation.

We continued on down a gravel road and I'm beginning to get a little nervous. We were going through big woods on both sides of the road that had been logged out. All of a sudden he took a left turn down a logging trail and on through the woods. We went down a long ridge, dodging stumps and tree tops. I'm thinking "Floyd you have done it now." I mean I was <u>S-C-A-R-E-D</u>.

Ahead I saw a camper like you put on a pickup truck. It was set up on concrete blocks. He stopped and said "You stay here." Not me boy! I went with him. I wanted to see exactly where he was going, what he was getting and mostly what he was going to do.

He never went into the camper. I was relieved. He went around it to the back. Right behind the camper under a small tree stood not one but two large Sears tool chest with drawers on the bottom and portable tool boxes on the top. Both were almost new and were full of all kinds of tools. He took the larger box and two drawers full of tools. Back up the ridge we went and into town to get the new bearing. We got back to my truck and had the new bearing installed in about one hour. He knew what he was doing.

I asked, "What do I owe you?" He said, "Maybe just a little gas money, that's all." I said "The mechanics in town don't work for nothing and neither should you." I paid him and was on my way. I hope I run into him again some time.

THE MOP MAN

I have a customer named Bill who I have been selling to for a long time. I ran into Bill several years ago and he told me he had a store and would like for me to supply him with bait.

I started stopping but I hardly ever saw Bill. His wife and another lady worked in the store and I had gotten to know them well. One day I entered the store and there was Bill and his wife and the other lady. Bill came straight to me and said, "You go back there and you pick up that display of mops and get them out of my store and refund all my money!" I said "Yes sir" and went to the back of the store.

I heard his wife whispering, "Bill, that's not the mop man that's the bait man." Bill came back and apologized profusely. We all had a good laugh. They still laugh and call me "Mop Man."

BILL

I had another customer named Bill, who was a rare bird. He moved into a house in a quiet farm neighborhood and built the front two rooms into a bait shop. He lived in the back of the house. Out to the side of the house he had a garden. He sold bait and raised a garden for a couple of years. He then decided he needed a little boost to his income so he applied for a license to sell beer.

Several of his neighbors objected to the beer board. His closest neighbor objected. There was a law in that county if a neighbor's house was within a specified number of feet, I think one hundred, and the neighbor objected the permit was denied.

Old Bill missed it by about ten feet. He was ill. A few weeks later I stopped by Bill's place and his house had been moved about thirty feet and was setting in his garden. He was under the house hammering and jacking for dear life trying to get a foundation under it.

I asked, "Bill, why did you set your house right in the middle of your garden?" "Do beans grow better if they've got a house on top of them?" He never did answer me. He thought he had beat the rap.

He got the foundation built and got his plumbing replaced, a new electric line and the whole nine yards. He was twenty feet over the limit. He applied for his beer license again. Guess what! His neighbor added a thirty foot carport. No beer!

THE MYNAH BIRD

I had a customer named Charlie a while back. Charlie was a likable sort of guy and was usually easy going. He would become a little fractious sometimes when the heat was on. His store was on a road that led to the dump. He told me one day if it weren't for the dump he probably could close but the guys that hauled the trash spent quite a bit of money there.

One hot summer day I was in his store and business was booming. Charlie didn't have any help. I had already put in his bait and was waiting to get paid. There was a man at the gas pumps blowing his horn to get the gas pumps turned on. The phone was ringing and there was a loud mouth over in the corner playing a pin ball machine. Three guys from the dump had ordered bologna sandwiches. One wanted bologna with cheese, one wanted double bologna and no cheese and the other wanted a big slice of onion. Behind the counter was a big cage with an old Mynah bird in it. He was feeling good. He was screaming and whistling and jumping around like a monkey.

Charlie didn't know where to jump next. The heat was on. It was all getting to him. I knew somebody was going to catch it.

Charlie laid down the stick of bologna and turned to the bird cage, "Shut up you son of a bitch or I'll wring your neck." The Mynah bird jumped behind a towel that was hanging in the cage and peeked out. All you could see was his beak and one eye. Everything calmed down.

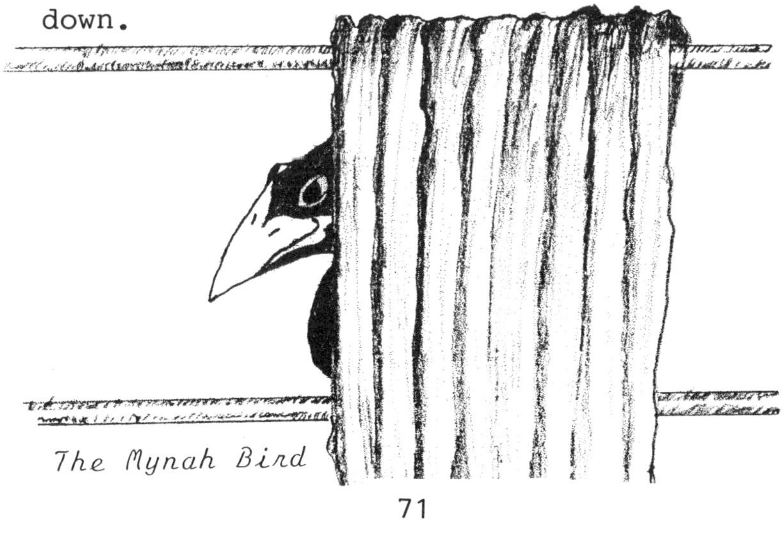

The Mynah Bird

"SPEEDO" AND THE CRUD

On another day I was in this store and one of the trash haulers was in the store. Now he was a sight to see. He had long bushy hair and a big bushy beard. His hair and his beard were nasty. He was nasty. His clothes and his shoes were all worn and dirty. He looked and smelled like he hadn't had a bath in weeks. Now on top of all this he had a terrible cold. He was a mess.

The lady running the store was very nice and was somewhat sympathetic. She said "Speedo, you seem to have caught a cold." He said "Naw it's the crud. Them younguns of mine brought it home from school and give it to me. I'm going home tonight and give it to the old lady."

THE COFFEE TRAIN

I came up on a railroad crossing one day and a train was stopped on the tracks. Just before you get to the railroad there is a cross road.

This road runs parallel to the railroad for quite a distance. The train was headed to the right. Down the road which turns to the right there is a store. While waiting for the train to move, I pulled down to the store. A man named Neal owned the store.

As I started to enter the store a man came out carrying a cup of coffee in each hand. I opened the door for him to come out. He went down a path and through some bushes to the train still setting on the track. He set one cup of coffee on a flat rock and climbed up in the train with the other. The train started to move. When the caboose got even with the cup of coffee setting on the rock, the train stopped again. The man in the caboose climbed down and got the cup of coffee. The train went on down the road. The traffic up at the crossing started to move.

I went in and asked Neal if I had really seen what I thought I had seen. He laughed and said "That's the coffee train. They stop here all the time."

ON THE ROAD

It seems that just about everybody has trouble hauling hay. I have seen hay spilled on the road everywhere. One load I remember very well. I met an old farmer pulling a wagon with a tractor. It was late one afternoon and he had a hard day. Just about everything he was wearing was wet with sweat except the galluses on his overalls. As I met him I noticed he only had two rolls of hay right on the front of his wagon. As I rode on down the road about a mile I saw where he had pulled across a small ditch to get up on the road. The rest of his load had rolled off and was laying in the ditch. The bad thing about it was he probably didn't know about it until he got all the way home.

On one of the roads I travel there is a big rounding curve. This curve really is fun when you hang into it at just the right speed. One day one of the good ol' boys up there was coming around the curve hauling a load of logs. When he got all the way around the curve he didn't straighten out and go on down the road, he just kept holding and went off down through the woods. I didn't see this happen but I was up there the next day while they were winching the truck out. They had traffic all backed up and everybody was watching. One of the locals up there asked the guy driving the truck why he didn't straighten out when he got around the curve. He said "Well I was hangin' into it so good, when I got around I just kept on hangin'" and he said "I was drunk too and you know how that is."

One rainy day I was driving on a two lane paved road where a bridge was being repaired. One lane of the bridge had been closed and a red light had been installed on each end to control traffic. The road leading to the bridge was down a long hill. I was sitting at the red light at the bottom of the hill waiting for it to turn green. While waiting, I looked in my rear view mirror and coming down at me was a big straight job Coca Cola truck. He was coming at about forty miles an hour, backwards. He was doing some kind of number, swapping ends and everything, so I decided to run the red light and give him room to do it. Luckily, he got it straightened out and we both crossed the bridge safely.

He followed me closely for about three miles to a small grocery store. I went on by and watched in my rear view mirror as he entered the parking lot of that store, backwards.

I often wonder if he was having a bad driving day or if he drives that way all the time.

THE SACK OF SEED POTATOES

I remember a store I sold to several years ago. There was a man who had a real good job in town. His wife didn't work outside the home so he decided it would be good if she could open a store not too far from where they lived. He rented an old store building and stocked it with just enough stuff so she could open and gave her the keys. She seemed to think he really didn't care about a profit but mostly wanted to provide her something to do.

One winter day I stopped in and she told me she was not selling much. She had a good sense of humor and often laughed about her plight in the store business. She told me she had told her husband she thought maybe they ought to close the store. She said he thought a minute and said "You know winter will be over before long and then people will be getting out and planting gardens and then you should really start doing good." She said, "I asked him just how much profit do you think I can make off of one sack of seed potatoes?"

DARLENE

A lady named Darlene called me one day and said she had opened a store and wanted me to bring her some bait. I told her I would come and talk to her about it. Her husband had built a small store right beside her house. It was only about ten feet off the road. It was, back in the country.

Darlene was a most interesting lady. She spoke the most fluent country I have ever heard. She should be in the movies. She was charming and she was genuine, she was for real.

I sold Darlene bait for three or four years. Each year her business grew. I enjoyed selling to her and I loved to hear her talk.

I stopped one day and she was out beside the store with a big stick. She had seen a snake and decided since it wasn't a rattler she wouldn't kill it. I asked her if there were rattlesnakes around. She got big eyed and said "Yeah buddy!" "They's a big one and a little one in the walls of that trailer you see yonder in the holler. You can tell their size by the way they buzz." She said "Them folks got younguns sleepin' on the floor too."

One day Darlene told me she "Wuz a thankin' I might have a yard sale." She asked if I would come. The sale was to start on Thursday. I always ran her on Thursday so I told her I would be there. She told me she had a bunch of junk she was going to move out. When I got there Thursday morning I could not believe what I saw. She had the good junk. She had an antique dough bowl hewn from a poplar log, a cedar water bucket and a Daisy churn. She had a crock churn with a well worn dasher, no doubt she had used for years, a pitcher and bowl and several hand made quilts. She had an antique, mahogany table that was set full of antique platters and a sewing box full of thimbles. Her yard was full of collectable items. All were priced far below their actual value.

I explained that she had her things priced too low. She said "It's just a bunch of junk, I'm tard lookin' at it." She assured me she just wanted it to go. I bought as much as I could get on my truck. Some of it I still have and treasure highly.

Darlene built her inventory from a few grocery items to everything you could imagine. She had groceries, bait, hardware, household items and eventually she added a feed store. People came from everywhere to buy cow feed and hog feed. She worked hard to keep whatever people wanted.

One day I went in and I sensed something was wrong. Darlene was not laughing and cheerful which was unusual. After we had talked a while she told me she was closing the store. She reached under the counter and pulled out a box. She said "This is what got me." "These folks won't pay me like they said they would." She had a box full of charge tickets and bad checks. What some of these people did to her was a shame. She was too good and too naive. Darlene deserved much better than this.

THE LEAKING ROOF

I sold bait to an older couple who had an old store. Over a period of several years the building really got in bad shape. In the rear of the building where they kept the bait you could actually look through the floor right down into the basement. When it rained the roof leaked something awful. They set pans, tubs, and cups all over the floor to catch the water.

Up front around the checkout counter there were several big brown stains on the floor caused from years of leaks. One day during a downpour the old man said, "Maw, we got a new leak." She asked "Where Paw?" He pointed to a big wet spot on the floor in front of the candy rack. She said, "NO, Paw that's been there three years." He got up and went over to the big spot as big as a tub that had been there three years. Just to the right of it about six inches he pointed to a wet spot about the size of a coffee cup and said "Here's the NEW leak."

THE UGLY YOUNGUN

I have sold bait to one family as long as I have been in business. This family consists of two brothers and their wives and their children.

M.A. and Johnnie Bell have three daughters. John and Juanita have one son and one daughter. I have sold to this family in four separate locations.

One day my wife, Betty, was riding with me and we were getting ready to leave Ms. Johnnie Bell's store. Betty asked me how many younguns Ms. Johnnie Bell had. I told her she had three girls. I said "She has one grown and married, one that works in the store and the little freckled up, UGLY one that's bouncing the ball off the side of the house over there is her youngest."

That was a BIG mistake!! I should not have said that. She dressed me down good. "Don't you dare call her ugly, She is just precious, a little darling." You see, Betty is nice, she likes younguns even when they're ugly.

"Ugly" Youngun

It took a while, but I talked my way out of that one because I was really only kidding. She was cute as a button, a little doll and she still is.

THE BEAUTIFUL LADY

John and Juanita have a son named "Bino." Now "Bino" is apt to say anything to anybody at any time.

One day I was in "Bino's" store and as I went to the checkout counter to collect for the bait I had put in I couldn't help but notice just in front of me there was a beautiful lady. I mean she was beautiful. She was a ten.

She had beautiful blond hair. Every curl was shining like silk and lay perfectly in it's place. She had beautiful blue eyes that sparkled as she smiled. Her teeth were as white as pearls, straight and even and perfect in every way. She had lips as red and smooth as the petals of a rose. Her skin was as smooth as a newborn baby. Her body was perfectly shaped, even down to her feet. She had expensive jewelry and clothes befitting to a princess. She was a sight to behold.

As she stepped up to the checkout counter, the only thing she had was a five dollar bill in one hand and a twist of King Bee chewing tobacco in the other. She laid both on the counter. "Bino" took the five and handed her back her change and the pack of chewing tobacco. As she started to leave "Bino" asked, "Can I get you a cup to spit in?"

"Bino" and the Beautiful Lady

RUN WHILE YOU CAN

Most of the remarks and comments I have heard around my stops over the years have all been made just in fun. I have, however, walked into a hornet's nest a couple of times. I once sold to a bait shop in an area where there were two groups of people that were not really fond of each other. Occasionally I had detected a comment that bore this out.

One day I was there and the shop was full of people. Most of them I didn't know. I certainly did not know which were from down on the creek and which were from out on the ridge. A man walked in and started talking to the woman behind the counter. The woman asked, "How's your daughter?" The man said, "She's fine, she just gets a little out of hand now that she is courting age."

The woman, in a very loud voice said, "She will be all right just as long as you keep her away from the creek." "The people down there are a sorry bunch. All they do is drugs and sex." She said, "The brothers do their sisters, the fathers do their daughters." I started easing toward the door. She said, getting louder, "They don't do it just for fun either, they make babies doing it. That's why they're all cross-eyed, club-footed and retarded down there."

By now, I'm not easing anywhere, I'm RUNNING. You get involved in conversation like that and somebody pulls out a 45 automatic and decides to have an ethnic cleansing, you're in big trouble. It can ruin your whole day.

CHICKEN LIVERS

Sometimes driving and delivering can become tiring, especially in the hot summer time when the days are long and hot. I remember one such time several years ago I had gotten tired and needed a break. I was over near Dale Hollow lake where I had a fishing camp at the time. I decided to go by the camp and fix some lunch.

The camp was a narrow mobile home with a screened porch added to the front. I went in and turned on the air conditioner. The only thing I could find to cook was a pack of frozen chicken livers.

I put the livers in a skillet and turned the stove on low to let them thaw. I sat down on the couch in front of the air conditioner and waited. It was 12:00 o'clock.

After the livers thawed, I battered them in flour and put them back on the stove to cook. I decided I would be a little more comfortable if I went on back to the bedroom and laid down on the bed.

I woke up at 3:00 o'clock. The livers looked like little lumps of coal. I threw livers, skillet and all out in the yard. NO lunch!

I rushed on through the rest of my route as fast as I could. I got home about 9:00 o'clock that night. My wife Betty, asked, "Where HAVE you been?" I think I told her about a year later.

HUSH PUPPY 'POSSUM

I have a lot of fond memories of that old camp. I remember not long after the liver episode I went over there for a couple of day's fishing with my long time friend and fishing buddy, Jackie Lee. We had fished hard the first day and had a good day. We decided to have fish, hush puppies, potatoes and slaw for supper.

Jackie always liked to cook so I cleaned the fish and peeled the potatoes and sat down to watch. The fish were cooking and he began to make the hush puppies. He reached for the salt, not the shaker but the big box that says "When it rains it pours." Now I thought

Too Much Salt

I saw what I saw but I thought he can see better than I, because he was much closer. He really put the salt to the hush puppies.

They were so salty they would curl your lips. The fish and potatoes and slaw were really good. We had two or three pieces of fish and most of the hush puppies left. I threw the left over fish and hush puppies out in the yard beside the back steps. I went back inside to do the dishes.

When we got ready to go to bed we both went out to check the boat, put up our fishing rods and turn out the porch light. We both noticed that a 'possum had gotten all the fish and hush puppies.

I talked to Jackie about this recently and he remembers it exactly as I did. Some time during the night, that 'possum brought all the hush puppies back. Too much salt!

THE BIG BULL DOG

I have watched a lot of dogs chasing cars and trucks and often wondered what they would do if they caught one. I had a stop where I had to go down a bumpy gravel road to get to a boat dock. Right beside the road there was a big dog pen. In it stayed a big bull dog. Now he was really big. He was the kind you see on the hood of a Mack truck. For some reason he really wanted to get to my truck. As I slowly bumped down the road he would go wild. He would run back and forth the full width of the pen. When he got to a corner of the pen he would climb almost to the top of the corner post, growling and screaming and barking all the time. He would then fall back and run back to the other end of the pen.

One day as I started down the road I noticed there was a second bull dog in the pen. The other dog was smaller and not nearly as fast. The smaller dog was trying to copy the big dog. Back and forth they started. The big dog was faster and got to the corner first. He turned around and started back to the other corner. About middle way of the pen they met head on. the big dog ran all over the smaller dog. Back and forth they ran. Their timing was all off. Each time they hit head on in the middle of the pen.

One day after I had gone down the road past the pen, I parked my truck and went down the path which went down the river bank and led out to the boat dock. I had put in their bait and was ready to go back up the path to my truck.

I noticed all the barking and screaming and growling had stopped. I looked up the hill at my truck and right beside the driver's door sat the big bull dog. He was looking down at me. He was smiling and licking his lips. I could imagine what the front page of the next "COUNTY CORNICLE" would read. "BULL DOG EATS BAIT MAN."

The lady who owned the dock and the bull dog assured me he would not bite. She went with me up the hill. Sure

The Big Bull Dog

enough, the big bull dog was a sugar lump. All these months of barking and growling and trying to get out of that pen, all he wanted to do was pee on my tires.

THE SUNKEN BOAT

I called on another boat dock one morning several years ago. I remember I had a truck load of bait, fish were biting, birds were chirping and I knew I had a busy day ahead. This particular dock was a big dock with the office and bait house out a long ramp, far from the parking lot. As I pulled onto the parking lot the owner of the dock and a couple of other guys were trying to pull a sunken ski boat out of the ramp with a small pickup truck. The dock owner told me to go out to the office and see how much bait they had. I went and came back and told him how much they had. He was still trying to pull the sunken boat up the ramp. I was waiting for him to tell me how much bait he needed. He pulled the sunken boat forward with the little truck. As the boat and trailer came up out of the water the truck spun and bucked and jumped. The boat full of water was just too much for the little truck.

I was in a hurry so I thought if I help him get the boat out then he will tell me how much bait he needs. I got a chain, from behind my seat, backed down the ramp and hooked on to his truck. I pulled the little truck, trailer, and boat full of water up in the parking lot.

The water in the boat still did not drain. He reached in and fumbled around down in the boat full of water and finally came up with a sock which was caught in the drain hole. I'm thinking, "Good, now how much bait is he going to need." We all stood there and watched as about a thousand gallons of water drained out. He finally turned to me and said, "You know, I think we have enough bait until you come back next trip."

SUSIE AND MISSY

After I had sold to U.L. about two years, he told me he had about all of the bait business he wanted. He had sold out. A couple from Maryland had bought his shop.

The new owners moved in. They had two little girls that were eight and ten years old. They were little dolls. I made a note that said "Susie blue, Missy brown." Until I could remember who was Susie and who was Missy, I kept the note to remind me that Susie was the little girl with blond hair and blue eyes and Missy was the little girl with blond hair and brown eyes.

After several stops in the store, one day I jokingly told their mother, while they stood by and listened how I had three teen-age boys I would trade for the two little girls. She just laughed and said "No deal."

This triggered a fantasy in the little girl's minds. It was the start of a make believe game. I became their "Daddy number two." They played out their parts so well, it all became so real, you guessed it, they became my daughters.

They started spending two or three days with us at Christmas. The first Christmas we put up and decorated a second tree. We shopped and made pictures with Santa Clause. We rode around, made pictures and did the things little girls like to do.

Over the years to come we went boating, had cook-outs, went fishing and celebrated birthdays. Susie is the older of the two. She liked to go on routes with me in the summer. When school would start in the fall I would plan my route so I would get to their shop after they had gotten home from school. They were special kids but they are not kids any more. Time has a way of getting away. They are both grown and each has a little boy and a little girl of their own.

We still get together for Christmas and to celebrate birthdays. They have been a big part of my life. I love them a lot and I always will.

THE JOHNNY CASH HOUSE

Over in Jackson County I had a customer whose name was Frank. His wife's name was Edna. Now old Frank really did like a joke or a prank as long as it wasn't on him. Over the years he pulled a couple of good ones on me.

One day I entered his store and he called me over to the side, and said, "I've been buying bait from you for a long time. Most of what I bought from you, I bought because I felt sorry for you." He said "You wear pants with your knees sticking out and your shoes are all worn out." He said, "There's a guy who lives down your way that came up here last week and he told me you have a big house and you are rich," I said, "Wrong, elephant breath."

I assured him that I had very little and my house was very modest. Over the next year gasoline went from 40¢ a gallon to $1.40 a gallon. Interest on borrowed money went to twenty per-cent, inflation was twenty per-cent.

Every time I went out on a route something had gone up. It was awful.

Old Frank never let up. Every time worms went up a nickel a cup or minnows went up a dime old Frank would set in, "You adding a room on that big house or is it a swimming pool?" For two years he bugged me about my house.

One Christmas while Susie and Missy were visiting we rode around and made some pictures. We went to Johnny Cash's house and made several pictures from different angles and they all turned out like the cover on a magazine. They were magnificent. I could not wait to get back up to see old Frank.

I really set him up. I told him about my two little girls I had gotten to know and how they had come to visit during Christmas. I said "Let me run to my truck and I'll show you some pictures."

He flipped through the pictures of Susie and Missy, our Christmas tree, some geese on the lake, a hot air balloon we found and then came the Johnny Cash house. The winding driveway, the limousines, swimming pools, the bath houses, rock gardens, flower beds and the lake. Each picture just kept getting better. It was nearly too much for Frank. He asked "Is this it?" I smiled and nodded. He chewed on his cigar and his face began to glow. His blood pressure must have shot up to two hundred, on the low side. He was in pain.

He asked "How do you find time to take care of all that yard?" I told him I did as much as I could and had a yard man about three days a week to do the rest. I could look at him and tell I had done good. I changed the subject and chatted a few minutes and left.

About two weeks later a man who worked at Frank's store asked me if I still had the pictures of my house. I couldn't lie to him so I called him aside and told him it was a joke and how I had laid one on Frank.

To this day Frank claims he knew better all the time but he didn't, I got him good.

YANKEES SOUND FUNNY

I went into a boat dock once carrying a case of worms on my shoulder. I set them on the floor and started putting them in the rack where they belonged. The man working at the dock was always pranking with me so he yelled over at me and said, "Hey worm man, You ever eat any worms?" I said "No, I never have, but every time I pick up a newspaper I read about the yankees eating them. They put them in cookies and casseroles and everything. They eat them all the time." As I stood up and turned around there were these two behemoth, burly yankees looking down at me. They just laughed and said "Hi Guy" as I left in a hurry.

I have had a lot of friends who were yankees. I liked them all, they are mostly good people, they just can't talk. I remember when Susie and Missy's mother, first moved here from Maryland, she was a riot. I mean she couldn't say anything. It was real strange, they could talk but she couldn't.

A few years back I took a trip up through the north east and over into Canada. I soon learned, I was the one who sounded funny.

While there, we went on a tour through an old castle. After the tour we walked around the grounds surrounding the castle. There, we found some very pretty and somewhat tame black squirrels. I decided to feed them. I went to a gas station nearby to get some peanuts.

I entered the station and started to look around. Two very neat and attractive ladies came over and asked if they might help me. They sounded as if they had learned to speak English from the queen herself. I said, "Yes, I'm looking for some peanuts." That's all I said. They looked at each other and began to laugh.

One of them then asked, "Why might you be wanting peanuts?" I said, "I found some little old squirrels over there at the castle and I just thought It would be a fun thing to do to go back over there and feed 'em some peanuts." They started cracking up. One asked, "What kind of peanuts do you want?" I asked "What kind y'all got?" She said "We don't have any but could you please stay and talk to us for a while?" I said "No, I got to find some peanuts."

LEONARD AND MS. HATTIE

Most stores or businesses have a hard time when they are first started. I remember one such store being built several years ago. The man who built it ran it for about two years and then had a run of bad luck and closed. It stayed closed about two or three years. Every time I passed, it always seemed such a waste.

One day I passed and the doors were open. The store was open again. I stopped to meet the new owners. A man named Leonard and his wife, Hattie were busy moving in, cleaning up and stocking shelves. They had bought the property.

Over the next few years they worked hard, selling groceries, gas, bait, and hardware. Ms. Hattie made lots of sandwiches. The farmers came for sandwiches at lunch time and the fishermen gathered to tell lies.

One day I went in and Ms. Hattie was not her usual cheerful self. The night before they had a break-in. The thieves took all of their candy, most of their cigarettes and a lot of cold drinks. They scattered stuff all over the floor. Now Ms. Hattie had gone home a little early the night before, leaving Leonard to close. She had been the first one in the store the next morning, after the break-in.

She started describing her feelings and thoughts when she entered the store that morning. She said she thought, "Leonard sure made a mess in the floor last night." "Leonard must have sold a lot of cold drinks after I left." "Ummm, he had a heck of a run on cigarettes too." "Huh, Must have been a bunch of kids in, he sold all the candy too." She said, "I'm thinking, Leonard really had a run on stuff."

I noticed Ms. Hattie was getting tears in her eyes. I knew exactly how she felt. I knew the disgust, the hurt and the violation she must have felt. I also remembered how she was extremely good natured and I knew she could take a joke.

I said, "Hold it Hattie, you seem to be having some difficulty articulating exactly what happened to you. I believe what you are trying to say is If you were any dumber than you are, you never would have figured out that you had been robbed."

"PEACHES"

I had a customer several years ago who sold bait right off her front porch. She was an elderly lady and was not able to do much else. She had a lot of fishermen who would circle around in her front yard, pick up some bait, and be on their way to the lake. Her whole front yard was parking lot, and turn around. She had a grandson she was raising who was about eight years old when she started selling bait.

The first stop I made after her grandson got out of school for the summer, he came out to the truck to check things out. He was a cute little cotton headed, blue eyed boy. He had been playing in the yard and was hot and sweaty. I flipped open my drink chest and asked, "Would you like to have a cold drink?" Quick as a flash he said "Make it a NE-HI Peach." I gave him all the drinks I had so he could sip along the next day or two. All of them were NE-HI Peach.

The next trip, my wife, Betty, was with me. As we pulled into the front yard, out of the house and off the porch and across the yard came the little boy. I told Betty, "Watch this." Before the truck had stopped, he said, "Hey! I'm out of Peach!!" After that we nick-named him "Peaches."

Through-out the summer, "Peaches" and I became good buddies. Summer and fall passed and Christmas came. I went to pick up Susie and Missy to spend a few days with us before Christmas. We stopped by to visit with "Peaches" and take him something on our way home.

First thing, "Peaches" asked, "What

are you doing with these girls?" I explained and he said "That's fine, next summer I want to go on a route with you and spend the night with you." I promised him he could.

The next summer I asked his grandmother and his daddy. They said he could go. His dad told me, "You'll never be able to handle him." I just laughed. I couldn't imagine that I couldn't handle a nine year old boy.

"Peaches" was ready to go. I picked him up early Thursday morning. We had a good day Thursday and a cook out that night. The next day I had a long hard day ahead. For "Peaches" it was going home day. The entire day he was totally a different kid.

Our first stop was to get fuel before we started the long day. When I went to the counter to pay for the fuel "Peaches" pitched down a deck of cards, a pair of adult sunglasses and a man sized cowboy hat. He instructed the lady "Add it all together, he will pay." I said "I will not! put it back."

He got worse as the day wore on.

He begged for money from everybody, he played pin-ball machines, punched punch boards, he did everything.

I needed a part for my John Deere tractor so I stopped at a John Deere dealer to get the part. In their show room they had some very expensive models of their big tractors. He grabbed up the biggest of the bunch and told the man at the counter "Cut us a deal and we'll take this too." I said "Put it back."

At the end of the day I was whipped. I carried him back home and his dad met us in the yard. He asked, "How did it go?" "Quickly "Peaches" said, "NO problems, I was real good, no trouble at all, a real good trip, right Floyd?" I just laughed. His dad said, "Boy, you didn't even give the man a chance to answer!" As I left we were both just shaking our heads.

Ms. NANCY

Many people have claims to fame or some kind of record to brag about. I have had a customer who would probably not admit and certainly would never brag about it but she has counted more minnows than anybody alive. Now I don't mean to suggest that she has sold more by the scoop or by the net full or weighed more by the pound but Ms. Nancy has counted one, two, three, four, more minnows than anybody, anywhere. She has bought from three generations of our family and sometimes with the fourth generation riding in the truck.

I remember when my son, Allen had joined the business and was running to Ms. Nancy's shop. One Saturday morning, he had gone to run the route she was on. I looked out the front window and saw his truck returning to our lot as the phone was ringing. Ms. Nancy was on the phone. She said in an urgent voice, "I need some minnows." I told her we would be there soon. She was thirty miles away.

I hurried back to the minnow shed

to see why Allen had skipped her. He said he had not skipped her but had sold her fifty pounds of minnows just two hours earlier. We quickly loaded the truck and back he went again. Fifty pounds of crappie minnows will count out about fifteen hundred dozens. She had the most unique way of counting minnows that I have ever seen. She had a sheet metal pan which was about four inches deep and about twenty inches square with a down-spout in the corner. The down-spout was placed in the minnow bucket and then minnows were poured into the pan. With a small wooden paddle she counted and pushed the minnows into the down-spout and into the bucket with much speed and accuracy.

Ms. Nancy loves people and likes to work as much as anyone I have ever known. She has operated her shop from early morning until late at night for as long as I have known her. With her sheet metal box and her little wooden paddle she has counted millions upon millions of minnows.

She smiles and laughs and she talks.

She greets every customer with a smile and never meets a stranger. She loves the young and the old and the in between. If you asked her about the millions of minnows she has counted she probably would pass it off as a joke. She would never claim credit for anything but to the many thousands who have the pleasure to know her, she has been a joy and a friend. I am a lot better for having known her.

Mr. R.D.

I have always tried to be careful while driving, trying to avoid running over animals in the road. I go out of my way to avoid hitting even a snake. One day I had made all of my stops and was driving on a country road when out of nowhere came two big dogs. They had hid in some weeds alongside the road and when I got close they jumped out in the road in front of me. I hit one of them with the front and back wheels. I stopped and went back where the old dog lay. There was no doubt about it, he was stone dead.

I looked around and there was a barn on one side of the road from where the dog had come. On down the road about a hundred yards on the opposite side of the road, was a farm house. I went down to the house and knocked on the door. An elderly lady came to the door. I explained that I had run over a dog back up the road and was wondering if it might belong to her. She pointed down the road on past the house and said, "The dog belongs to the man coming there, you'll have to deal with him." The man was coming in a fast walk. He was a big elderly man with piercing eyes. He looked back and forth, at me and then to my truck in a puzzled look.

As he neared the house I said, "Sir, I'm sorry, but I think I have killed your dog." He said "I'll go look." As we went up the road to where the dog lay, he asked, "What are you doing in these parts?" I told him I was a bait dealer. As I continued to apologize, I offered to help him bury his dog. I knew that I had not killed just a dog or a squirrel or a groundhog, but I had killed the old man's friend. I felt really bad. As we reached the spot where the dog lay, again I offered to help him bury it. He said "No, I'll take care of him." With that, he picked the dog up by the back legs and heaved it down in a ravine on the low side of the road. The old dog disappeared down in the briars and honey suckles. I apologized again and went to my truck and left.

Several years passed and my friend Susie had grown up and married. She told me one day that she and her husband had bought a house. She told me where the house was located. It was just up the road from where I had run over the dog. On the day she was moving in, I stopped for a short visit as I went through on my route. As I entered the garage, I noticed the man who owned the dog had stopped in for a visit with his new neighbor. Susie greeted me and said, "Oh, Mr. R.D. I want you to meet my friend, Floyd." As I shook his hand and said, "Good to meet you sir." he said, "I already know you, you're the one that killed my dog." I stayed a few minutes and left.

Several years passed and I started looking for a lot to build a fishing camp. I found a lot that was suitable and bought it. It was down the road, joining Mr. R.D. on the lower side of his farm.

One day I was clearing part of the lot and sawing some fallen trees into firewood. My youngest son, Charlie was helping me and we were down in the hollow below the road where the camp was to be built. I looked up on the hill and there was a pick-up truck. I only lacked about two cuts being through so I told Charlie to go up the hill and visit and I would finish sawing.

When I got to the top of the hill, the truck was gone. Charlie said, "That was your neighbor from up on the hill. His name is Mr. R.D." I told him my name was Charlie and that was my dad down the hollow sawing wood. He said he knew you, and you were the one who had killed his dog.

About a year later I finished my camp and I wanted to find out what my address was and put up a mailbox. I started hunting the post office. I drove over miles of back roads. I came up on a country store and stopped for directions. A mother and daughter were running the store. The daughter was about seventy years old.

I asked if they could direct me to the post office. The mother asked, "Why do you need to find the post office?" She then said, "We have stamps and envelopes." I explained how I needed to know my new address so I could get insurance on my house and put up my mailbox. She asked where the house was. I told her which road it was on. She asked exactly where it was. I told her it was about half way down the hill after you go around the big curve. She said, "Your place must join Mr. R.D." I said, "Yes it does." She said, "You must be the man who killed Mr. R.D.'s dog."

By now, I was beginning to get a little bent out of shape. I told them, "That was about twelve or fifteen years ago and I stopped and apologized and did everything I knew to do, and he still has bad feelings toward me about that dog. I couldn't help it. It was an accident." Quickly they both jumped up. "Oh no! You don't understand. The reason he was telling us about it, was because he really did appreciate your stopping to apologize when it would have been so easy to just drive on."

Mr. R.D. and his wife Marge have become such good friends since. A better neighbor you could never have.

NO FACILITIES

On many of the roads I have traveled, finding a public rest room is quite a problem. I remember one day I was about thirty or forty miles past due when I just pulled over on the side of the road. It was in the fall of the year and there was not much traffic on this particular road. I left my motor running and went to the front of the truck. I didn't even raise my hood like I was checking my engine, I just cut loose. I was standing there looking up at the most beautiful hill side I had ever seen. It was October and the trees were red and gold and brown and green and every shade in between. It was beautiful. As I stood there, looking up, admiring and enjoying the beauty of this hill, I completely forgot what I was doing. As I looked back down, I looked straight into a van full of gray haired ladies. They were cracking up.

MR. HATLEY

Many of our suppliers have been people we deal with over the phone but never actually meet. One of these was a black man from Mississippi. I talked to him hundreds of times over the phone but I never met him. He raised crickets and sold them throughout the south-eastern states. In the off season he would travel around and drop in to see his customers. I never knew when he was coming, so every time he came to see me I was gone. He passed away a few years ago. Of all the suppliers I have had, he was one of the best. If Mr. Hatley told you something, you could take it to the bank. He was a prince of a man. I truly regret never having met him.

RONALD AND WAYNE

Back in the early days we bought bait from some brothers and cousins and their in-laws over in the Carolinas. They all talked with a long mountain drawl and they all sounded the same.

Some of the things they did to each other was awful. Their names were Marvin, Ronald, Michael, Wayne and Charles.

For a long time I never really knew which ones were brothers and which were cousins. I didn't know if they were partners or competitors. You couldn't find out because you could ask any one of them and they would just laugh.

After I had gotten to know Ronald well I asked him one day "How many brothers do you have?" He said "There are four of us." I asked, "Are you all in the bait business?" He said, "No, there are three of us in the bait business and one rides a motorcycle."

As we sat and talked he told me he had been in the bait business sixteen years. He recalled that when he first started he had thirty five cents and a full pack of Phillip Morris cigarettes. He said after sixteen years he still had only about thirty five cents but he had managed to quit smoking.

One day I was talking to Wayne, who was one of the cousins and he was telling some of the things he had seen and heard. He said a bait dealer he knew that was not one of his clan had bought a load of night crawlers and paid sixty thousand dollars for the load. He carried them across the state and sold them for forty thousand dollars the same day.

About that time somebody came up and interrupted our conversation. The next thing I knew, Wayne was in his truck and gone. I never saw him again for about a year. I kept thinking about the guy and the load of worms. Just how dumb can you be.

The next time I saw him I asked, "How about the guy who bought the load of worms for sixty thousand dollars and sold them the same day for forty thousand dollars?" He said "Oh, I thought I told you, he paid for them with a hot check."

Ronald and Wayne should have been in the movies. If Warner Brothers had followed them around, I know they would have paid them more than they made selling worms. At one time they had an old truck that must have had a bazillion miles on it. They came to my place and started to unload a load of worms. They were carrying them all the way around the building to the back. I said, "Back in behind the building and it will be much closer." Wayne laughed and said, "We can't, reverse has been out on our truck about a month now."

They continued unloading and checking a box now and then to see if the worms were lively. Now there was something about a good box of worms that Ronald couldn't resist. He really did like to dig around in them with both hands.

When they finished unloading, Ronald said, "We didn't stop for breakfast this morning. I need a snack." He went to the cab of the truck and got a pack of snack crackers and a cold drink. The crackers were crushed like he had been sitting on them for days. His hands were as rough and dirty as elephant feet. He poured the cracker crumbs into his hand and started to eat. It was a sight to see.

One day I picked up a news paper and there as plain as day was a picture of Charles up in church, dancing around with an armful of rattlesnakes. I think Charles was a brother-in-law to Wayne. I couldn't get this picture out of my mind for quite some time.

A few weeks later in the paper was another story. Charles had been bitten by one of the big snakes and had died.

BORIS

Several years ago I was working around my shop and a man came to me and introduced himself. He said "My name is Boris. I would like for us to make business." I soon learned, he was in the business of selling night crawlers.

From the start, I became very fascinated with this man. He was very interesting.

Boris was a big man with a big smile. I soon learned he was a Bulgarian. At first I had difficulty understanding him but now I understand him well.

He was extremely intelligent, a hard

worker and a shrewd business man. I have had extensive business dealings with him. We have also had our share of disputes, some clashes and some bad times. We have spent many hours just talking. He has told me of his escape from Bulgaria and how he left his parents and friends behind to make his escape into the free world. It was many years before he could return to visit his aging mother.

He truly appreciated the simple things in life that most of us never notice or just take for granted. It was always amazing that as we talked he would comment about a cool breeze, a sunset, or even the wild flowers he had seen along the highway on his way down.

One day as we were talking he said, "Sometime I would like to go to your home, not to make business, but just to visit and see where you live."

The next trip he made to my shop I carried him to my home. He entered the house and became interested in the books, magazines and pictures. He spotted a picture of Susie and me that was made at her wedding. He said, "You never told me you had daughter!" I said, "She is not my daughter." He said, "Then she must be niece." I said, "No she is not my niece."

My friend, Susie, with me at her wedding

As he held the picture, he said "She is so beautiful, she is so happy, she is so full of life, who is she?"

I told him about how I had gotten to know Susie and Missy when they were little girls and how we had all the good times when they were growing up and how I had come to love them as if they were mine.

When I had finished, I noticed tears had welled up in his eyes. He stood there with his arms spread and his big hands open and upward as if he were holding all the treasures of the entire world, and he said, "Do you mean you HAVE, ALL OF THIS just because you sold their mother some worms?" I said, "Yes, I HAVE, ALL OF THIS, just because I sold their mother some worms."

As Boris left that day, he asked, "Maybe you could come to my home in Canada sometime, not to make business, but just to visit?" I promised him I would.

The next year we went to Canada. When we got to the town where he lived,

I called him. He said, "Give me about thirty minutes and I will drive across town and lead you back to where I live." We waited and when he showed up he was dressed in very nice clothes. He looked like a preacher.

He led us back to his home which was very comfortable and in a very nice neighborhood. He was proud. He had every right to be.

When I think of him, I can't help but think of the work he has done, the sacrifice he had to make and what he had to go through just to be able to sell worms. He is my friend and he always will be.

Boris passed away in October, 1998 after a long bout with cancer.

MILITARY PEOPLE

I have had several customers who have retired from the military. I remember one in particular. I never could get comfortable while I was around him. Not being a military person myself, I never knew exactly what was expected of me. Each time I entered his store he jumped to attention and saluted. After I had put in his bait and he had paid me, he would salute as I started to leave.

I always thanked him in as gracious a manner as I knew. It must have pleased him. I sold him lots of bait over a long period of time.

UNSOLICITED TESTIMONIALS

Just about everybody has run into unsolicited testimonials about the goodness and superiority of all kinds of products and things. I encountered a boy who was working in a bait shop once who was really big on the benefits of drinking lots of good well water.

Now from day one it was quite evident

"Elmo"

that Elmo's elevator didn't go all the way to the top. He acted like maybe he had been dropped when he was a baby.

On several occasions, Elmo had told me about how he drank lots of good, cold, well water. He said his father and his grandfather always drank lots of good well water. He was convinced it contributed to their good health, long life and well being.

One day he showed me his cup which he had hung conveniently near the minnow tank. "None of the chlorine and chemicals you get in city water for me," he proclaimed as he filled his cup from the stream of water entering the end of the minnow tank.

Having built a few of these tanks, I knew they were mostly large aquariums which were filled with water which was cooled and aerated and circulated over and over within the tank.

I suggested to him that what he was drinking was not what he thought, but was coming straight off the minnows. When I removed the top from the filter box and showed him he got sick.

MRS. "RED"

Mrs. Red told me one day she had heard about these tanks and would like to buy one for her minnows. I told her I would deliver one to her, which I did. I sold her the tank and showed her how to clean it and change the filters. She was extremely proud and kept it clean and in good shape as long as she stayed in business. When she went out of the bait business, I bought the tank back from her. I have bought and sold this tank several times since then. I have bought and sold it five times during the past twenty years. It is still in use today.

After Mr. Red passed away, Mrs. Red continued selling bait. Selling bait was all she had ever done. She sold several years after he was gone. She loved people and liked to hear fish stories and she liked to talk. After many years of selling, she had some serious health problems and had to quit. After she had taken down her "FISH BAIT" sign and quit selling,

I still went by to visit and "try" some of her cooking or a cup of coffee when I had time.

One day while I was visiting her she looked at me with her usual smile and said, "I got something I want to tell you." She said, "I never told anybody about this, not even my sons, but I want to tell you." She said, "I always wanted a nice diamond ring, but I never did have one." She continued, "A few years back I got to thinking about how I had always wanted one and never could get one so I prayed and asked God to give me one." She said she felt real bad about asking God for something like that but just a few days later she was cupping up some night crawlers and found one mixed in with all the dirt and worms. She smiled and showed me the prettiest little diamond ring. She said she cleaned it up and it fit perfectly. She said she had been wearing it ever since.

Mrs. Red had a lock box with a combination lock on it. Over the years when I was selling her bait she would sometimes open the box and show me her silver coins she had saved. She had quart fruit jars full of old silver dimes, quarters and halves. She had saved them for years and had several quarts of each. She had told me she was becoming concerned about having that much money at home.

A few months later I stopped by to visit her. She asked if I remembered seeing all her silver and I told her I did. She said she had carried it all to the bank a few months back. She went back to get it that week and they brought out all this paper money. She told them she wanted "Her" money back but they told her it didn't work that way.

She actually thought she was putting her coins in a safe deposit box. When I heard this I could hardly believe bank tellers who are supposed to be honest, decent people could have done this to this little old lady. Believe me, they did it.

One spring day I stopped by Mrs.

Red's for a visit. I knew this would be my last visit for a while for summer and the busy season was coming. She was very cheerful with lots to talk about. I knew she had an enlarged heart and some serious blood pressure problems. She laughed and talked and told me how some T.V. preacher had healed her and she had thrown out all her medicine. She said she was sending him money and he was strengthening her daily.

The next visit I made was late summer. Her neighbors told me she had passed away in the spring. She was a dear lady and a special friend. I'll always remember her.

KNOWING WHAT NOT TO SAY

Sometimes knowing what not to say is about as important as knowing what not to do. I used to sell bait to a drive-in package beer store. About all they sold was beer, rolling papers and night crawlers. I supplied the night crawlers. The turnover of help at this store was unreal. It seemed about every other trip there was new help.

One day I pulled into the parking lot and got out of my truck and started up to the drive-in window to take their order. As I approached the window, there was this quite attractive young lady smiling out at me. With a burst of unbridled arrogance, I said "Hello! You must be the new girl." She quickly replied, "Hell no, I own this place." I said, "Oh, excuuuuse me."

THE "DEER HUNTER"

Late one afternoon, I had finished my route and was going home on the interstate. The big gun portion of deer season had just opened that day. As I was driving, I noticed up ahead of me there was a nice buck coming across an open field headed toward the highway. I could tell by the way he was running he was going to cross. I stopped and pulled over to avoid the deer. There were cars everywhere. The deer crossed and one of the cars hit him just enough to spin him around and knock him down. Up he jumped and ran into a small patch of bushes in the median between the east-bound and west-bound lanes. A pickup truck quickly pulled to the left side of the road and the driver grabbed a deer rifle from the rack behind the seat. Into the median he ran after the deer. The deer ran to the east-bound lanes of traffic and turned and came back toward me. The "deer hunter" was shooting like crazy. Bullets were flying everywhere. He killed the deer. It fell not far from the front of my truck. I crawled out from under the dash of my truck and walked over to see what he had killed. It was a nice eight point buck.

As I approached the deer the guy that killed it came running up and said, "How about you helping me drag this deer down to my truck?" I said, "How about you dragging it yourself, that deer is about as illegal as you will ever kill." He said "This is the first chance I ever had to kill a nice deer like this." I told him if he got caught, it probably would be his last one. I got in my truck and left.

THE SANDWICH

One day I stopped in a country store where I sold bait. It was about lunch time. As I entered the store, I noticed a couple of loggers had stopped in for lunch. One of these men was standing in the middle of the store eating a ham and cheese sandwich. He was standing there with his eyes shut with a look on his face like I had never seen before. He was totally oblivious to everything else in the world except that sandwich. He was savoring every bite.

The lady behind the counter was watching me, watching him, and she asked, "Would you like a sandwich?" I said, "Yes ma'm." She asked what kind I wanted. I said, "I want one just like that man over there is eating." She smiled and started to build the sandwich. I went to the drink box and got a cold drink and then paid her for the drink and sandwich and started on down the road.

About the second bite I took, I realized why the old logger had his eyes shut. You talking about HOT!, I mean it was some kind of HOT. I threw that thing out the window, drank my cold drink and spent the next hour trying to cool my burning lips.

THE TALL FISH TALE

I have heard a lot of tall tales about fish that were caught or about the big ones that got away. Some are true and some make you wonder. Recently, I heard a tale that I have no reason to doubt.

A man who trades with one of the

shops I supply, caught a catfish that weighed twenty five pounds. He brought the fish in to get his picture made. He said he had caught a catfish one time that weighed thirty two pounds but he said he was much prouder of the smaller fish. When asked why, he said he was prouder of the smaller fish because it took him two days to catch it. He said when he hooked the fish it pulled and pulled and he never could get it to come up from the deep water. Finally the fish swam into a cave or hole in the bank and would not come out. He could feel the fish surging and pulling up in the hole but could not get it out.

He tugged at the fish until it was time for him to go home. He said he tied his line to a limb near the water's edge and left. When he came back the next day the fish had come out of the cave and he reeled it in.

THE FROG HUNTERS

Another story that happened at my retail shop many years ago is about a couple of frog hunters. One morning just after daybreak, two guys named Stan and Jerry came to my shop after a night of frog hunting. They had enjoyed a night of successful beer drinking and frog hunting. They must have had at least a hundred frogs and about that many beer cans in the back of a pickup truck. They had the frogs strung up on a long rope. They wanted me to make their picture, which I did. They wanted me to send it in to the local paper, which I didn't do. Two men can't catch six limits of frogs and then run it in the paper. They had a good time.

As they started to leave, Stan thanked me for making their picture. He said "We really had a good time. We would have hunted all night if it hadn't got daylight on us." He hesitated for a second and then said, "Well, you know what I mean." I said, "Yeah, Stan, you would have hunted all night if it hadn't got daylight on you."

LOST AT THE PAY-LAKE

I got a call from a man one day who owned a pay-lake. A pay-lake is a lake or pond where fish are brought in and released and then caught out by fishermen who pay a fee for fishing. The man explained to me that his lake was way out in the country but that it was a popular spot with many people coming to fish. He thought if he could get bait he could sell to fishermen coming to fish. He was right, he sold a lot.

To get to his lake he explained, when you get off the interstate you take a right and then go to a stop sign, then you take another right. Go to the next road to the left and take it. Go a few miles to a stop sign and take a left. Go a few more miles and look for a pay-lake sign which points down the road to the right, cross a creek and then up a hill and there I would find his lake on the left. I went right to it, no problem.

After making two or three trips back,

one day I wanted to get to the next county south of there. I asked the lady keeping the lake that day if there was any way I could get down into the next county without going all the way back to the interstate, which I knew was several miles north.

She said "Oh yes, go back out to the main dirt road and take a right instead of a left. Go to the next stop sign and take a right. Go to a fork in the road and take a right, then at the next cross road take a left which will lead you to the big highway and on into town." I made a note and followed her instructions and came out just as she said I would.

The next week I delivered bait to the pay-lake and headed up to the main dirt road and took a right and was on my way into the next county south, I thought. I had lost my note. I made a few rights and a few lefts and I drove on and on. I kept thinking I would see something familiar after a while. I never did. Even the crows and blue jays looked different. It was getting on up in the day. No doubt about it, I was lost.

As I drove on, I came up on a church where a full grown boy was cutting grass. I stopped and started walking over to where he was mowing. He stopped and came to meet me. "What can I do for you?" he asked. I replied, "I'm lost, can you tell me where I am?" He looked at me kind of funny and asked, "Do you mean right now?" I said, "I mean right now." He said, "You're in the church yard."

I started thinking what simple question I could ask next. I asked, "If I keep going down this road the way I'm going, where will it take me?" He said, "I don't know, I've never been down that road." I said "Oh I'm sorry, I thought maybe you lived around here." He said "I do, I was born over there," as he pointed across the road. He said, "When I go out, I always go out this way," pointing down the road from where I had come.

I got in my truck and turned around and started trying to find my way back.

As I drove I kept thinking about the boy. He must have been intellectually challenged, or to put it in bait dealer terms he was dumber than a worm.

I drove on several miles and started to feel much better when I got to where I could see the big trucks rolling down the interstate over on the next hill.

As I drove on, I started thinking how I had been a little hard on the boy in my thoughts, after all I was the one who was lost. I kept wondering why he had never been down the road that went right in front of his house. Maybe he didn't want to get lost.

I kept thinking about the two questions I asked him and the dumb answers I got. Then I thought, it's no big deal. A navy blue suit, a white shirt and a bright red tie and he could be vice-president.

TOO MANY CRICKETS

Dealing in live bait is a tricky business to say the least. Like produce or flowers or any perishable item you have to be careful in buying as well as selling. Every bait shop owner or bait dealer's constant dream is to buy exactly the right amount, so you don't miss any sales or you don't have a lot left over that you lose.

Crickets are raised commercially by growers who box them up daily and ship them to bait dealers who in turn deliver them to the shops that retail them. They are usually shipped through the mail in boxes that contain about a thousand crickets. They are sealed in the boxes which have screened vent holes. Each box has enough sliced potatoes enclosed to supply the crickets food and moisture for about three days. The first day is used in the mail coming to the bait dealer. This gives the bait dealer about two days to sell them to the retail shops.

A few years back, I remember it was

getting on down in the fall and cricket sales had begun to slow. For some reason I had gotten a little ambitious and bought enough crickets for everybody to have some. I had run all day and it was getting late in the afternoon and I had not sold a box of crickets all day. I was seething with self-pity as I approached my last stop of the day. This stop was a large commercial boat dock which was run by my friend Darwin.

I have sold bait to Darwin for as long as I have been in the business. He is an all right guy even though he still gets outside the lines when he colors. He got on my case about everything he could. When the fish didn't bite, it was my fault, when the weather was bad, it was my fault.

On this day as I entered the dock he had a pretty good audience, so he started on me. "Bait man, you are about as sorry as you can get. You must really work at it to be as sorry as you are." "You have let me run out of crickets again." "How many do you think I need to buy so I don't run out?"

I didn't answer, I just stood there and grinned. He continued, "How many crickets do you have on your truck?" I still didn't answer, I just shrugged my shoulders like I didn't know. He said, "However many you have, I'll take them all."

I went to my truck in a hurry. I mean I had crickets, I had cricket's mama! I couldn't believe it. Old Darwin wanted them all.

I rushed back to the dock and started dumping crickets. When I got through he had crickets in his box about a foot deep. I collected my money and headed home with an empty truck.

The next trip I went into the dock and Darwin was waiting for me. He said "Guess what!" I said "Let me guess, you ran out of crickets." He said, "There is something wrong with my cricket box." I went out to the bait room and checked and found a big rat had gnawed a big hole in the back of the box. There were crickets on the floor, crickets on the walls, they were on the broom, they were everywhere except in the box where they belonged.

I plugged the hole and put him in some more crickets.

MR. RAT

I thought this would be the end of Mr. Rat but not so. He managed to stay hid all winter but the next spring I started to see little signs that he was still around.

The bait room at this dock was a large shed that was floated out beside the main dock and retail area and was not open to the public. It was used to store the cricket box as well as a lot of junk. This made a perfect set-up for Mr. Rat.

One day as I opened the door to the shed and started across to see how many crickets they might need, the rat climbed out of the box of cricket feed which stayed on top of the cricket box. He darted off into the piles of junk to hide.

I got a good look at him. He was a big fat woods rat. He was red headed and had red sideburns. Each trip as

Mr. Rat

I opened the door and entered the shed, he would jump from the box of cricket feed and scramble to the piles of junk to hide.

We started playing a game. It was kind of like cat and mouse except it was "bait man and rat."

One day I opened the door very slowly. I walked quietly and slowly across the shed with my leather money pouch in my hand. I slammed the pouch over the hole in the corner of the cricket feed box which was a square box about like a shoe box. I had Mr. Rat inside. Thump, thump, around and around he went, inside the square box. Now that I had him, I didn't know what to do with him. I quickly started to the door to sling him out into the lake so he could swim to the bank and back into the woods where he belonged. As I crossed the shed, I stumbled and fell and shot the rat, box and all out the door as I fell. He ran like a greyhound, down the long ramp which led to the parking lot and on up into the woods. I never saw him again.

FISHING AND LYING

I have been taught, for as long as I can remember, about the wrongs and evil of lying and stealing. But, as is the case with most people, the vices and short-comings of other people always seem a lot worse than my own. This statement in itself may open way for discussion of the old controversy of whether there are degrees of sin.

I well remember when I was growing up there was a definite size and severity of a lie, one being the big black lie and the other being the little white lie. Later on into my adult life as I became involved in serious fishing, I became familiar with the fishing lie. The fishing lie falls in well below the little white lie, both in size and color. I can find no justification at all for any form of stealing or the big black lie. The little white lie is definitely serious, it just seems much more forgivable. I'm not sure the fishing lie carries any consequences at all.

Several years ago, my wife, Betty and I were getting ready to go to Lake Okeechobee, Florida to fish a few days. Out in front of our retail bait shop I had my truck and boat, fully loaded with fishing gear ready to go. Betty was gathering a few things for the trip. We were just minutes from leaving.

A group of fishermen were sitting around the wood-burning stove in the back of the shop. It was the middle of January and it was cold. The ground was frozen a foot deep. The temperature was about ten degrees and dropping fast with a hard wind coming straight out of the north. I mean it was cold. I had just put an arm full of wood in the stove and it was doing good.

We were all having a good time. We were enjoying an interchange of ideas and the free flow of intellectual discourse. More aptly put, we were bullshitting. Through the front door came our now departed friend, Stinson, may he rest in peace. Back to the stove he came, interrupting whoever thought they had the floor at the time. "By-grab, I want to know who has little enough sense to go fishing on a day like today!" he demanded. We just looked at each other. "By-grab, whoever owns that boat out there, had better have some good clothes!" he said, "It's cold out there."

I told him the boat belonged to me. I told him we were going to Florida where you could sit around in the sun, listen to the sea-gulls scream, eat oranges right off the tree and catch as many big crappie as you want. He said, "By-grab, I have heard around town about some of these trips you have made down there and what I want to know is how do you bring that many fish back?"

By now, I'm beginning to lean over and whisper. Pointing out toward the truck I said, "You put a layer of ice in the bottom of the truck bed and then you put a layer of fish, another layer of ice and then another layer of fish, and as long as you don't stack them any higher than the sides on the truck you can come on back with them."

Now I knew Stinson liked a good tip on where to catch a big fish or a lot of fish or any fish at all when the ground was frozen a foot deep. Out the door he went with a gleam in his eye.

Betty and I threw in a few extra hooks and sinkers and headed down the road.

The trip is seven hundred and thirty miles, so we drove about five hundred miles and got a motel room, after all this was a vacation, not a marathon. The next morning we drove on into Okeechobee.

The blizzard we had back home had pushed it's way all the way to south Florida. They had a forty degree drop in temperature and were at about thirty-five degrees. That kind of drop in temperature, along with the changes in barometric pressures, has a devastating effect on fish. I knew fishing was going to be bad for at least two or three days.

We came to fish, so we went on to the lake and launched our boat. The parking lot at the ramp serves a store, a dock and a restaurant so it is quite large. As I circled the parking lot looking for a double spot which would accommodate my truck and boat trailer I noticed a truck was following me. Finally, as I parked, the truck stopped directly behind me. As I got out to see what they wanted, out jumped old Stinson. He had driven straight through without stopping and had beat us down there. He was ready to fish.

He said, "I want you to meet my brother-in-law who lives here in Okeechobee, and by-grab I want you to tell him how you pack your fish to carry them back to Tennessee."

I began to think that a fishing lie might carry more consequences than I had originally thought and maybe even a lot sooner than I had anticipated. I began to wonder if I should try to explain the difference between the big black lie, the little white lie and the fishing lie which if viewed properly is almost invisible.

Luckily, I didn't have to explain.

His brother-in-law, upon hearing the tale from Stinson, had already told him he had been snookered. We all had a good laugh and went fishing.

We fished the first three days with very little success, which I expected. The cold spell hung on. Every where you went there were old men wearing cut-off britches and fur lined parkas, grumbling about the worst cold spell in fifty years.

Each day, I ran into Stinson at the ramp or out on the lake and tried to encourage him to wait out the cold spell. He was losing his patience. I knew that down there the weather can change over night. He fished the worst three days in many years and left for home without catching a fish.

The next day after he left the temperature jumped back up to seventy five degrees. The fish started biting like crazy. I started to feel guilty as we sat there in the sun, catching fish, listening to the sea gulls scream, and eating an orange now and then. But then I thought maybe his trip was not a total loss, after all he did get to hear the sea gulls scream and eat a few oranges.

When I got back home, several days and many fish later, I went out to the barber shop, where my friend Stinson hung out a lot. As I sat down in the barber chair, I asked my friend, John the barber, how Stinson liked his Florida fishing trip. I knew Stinson and John the barber were best fishing buddies. He replied, "Oh he hasn't been to Florida, he just left here and he didn't say anything about going." I said, "Yes, he went to Florida last week fishing." John the barber persisted, "Oh no!" "He has been in here every day for the past four days and he has not mentioned going to Florida." I guess one fishing lie deserves another. He had driven seven hundred and thirty miles to Florida, fishing, came back empty handed and denied he had ever been there at all.

LEARNING TO FISH

I have enjoyed fishing since I was very young. I started fishing in farm ponds and later I sneaked on to the creek and even the big river. I went fishing as often as I could, and fished for whatever was biting at the time.

After Betty and I married, she went fishing with me but somehow I felt she really didn't like fishing as much as I did. We fished for any kind of fish we could catch, but on days that were slow, she sat in the back of the boat and read a book.

After we got into the bait business, we felt a need to fish even more. Knowing what kind of bait and tackle to use is a big help in selling. A lot of this information comes easy if you just listen, some comes from years of fishing.

After many years of my fishing and her reading a book, we started fishing for blue gill. I noticed she became more interested, with the sport and excitement these little fish can bring, especially with light tackle. She started leaving the books at home.

One day about the middle of May we found a bed of big blue gill. They were bedding just a few feet from the

Catching Blue Gill

bank on a gravel bar that was about thirty feet wide. We were in our boat, casting crickets in toward the bank. When you cast a cricket and let it drop down into the bed, you would see a slight twitch on your line when you got a strike and then the battle was on. Blue gill fight harder, ounce for ounce, than any fish I have ever caught. This particular bed had some of the biggest we had ever found.

Betty was catching her share that day, she was having fun. She was jumping up and down in the boat, screaming and hollering and clapping her hands and just generally having a good time. It was a sight to see and hear.

After a while, I looked up in the woods and there, peeking out from behind a tree, was a little old man. He was grinning like a mule eating briars. He stayed a few minutes and watched and then disappeared back up into the woods. He stayed gone a short while and then came running back down the hill with a bucket of crickets in one hand and a fishing pole in the other.

We backed our boat out and eased away, giving him the spot, after all we knew several more spots on up the lake. We caught fish every where we went, we saw deer, we saw wild turkeys feeding near the lake, birds were chirping, the weather couldn't have been better. We went back to camp that evening and had a fish fry. Fresh blue gill are about as good as you can get. We had a fantastic day. After it was all over we talked about it and decided this was about the most fun we had ever had with our clothes on.

We have kept fishing through the years, learning every trick we could. Betty had gotten past the book reading, she had become a fisherperson. Fishing had become more than a pastime with her, it had become an obsession. It was serious business. We continued fishing, having more good days than bad. One day she got a wistful look in her eye as she looked across the lake and up into the hillside. She said, "I think when I die, I want to be cremated." And she said, "I want my ashes to be scattered up in Little Hurricane Creek."

I got this funny feeling. I knew I needed to get her home immediately and get her an appointment with my psychiatrist, as soon as I could, but for the life of me, I could not remember his name. So we just kept fishing, and fishing, and fishing.

I have learned, over time, that you can fish all day and catch nothing at all and it is still a good day. You count the things that count most. You count the beauty of a sunrise or a sunset, the serenity of a full moon. You count the spring showers or a summer breeze or a rainbow. You count the sighting of an eagle as it soars high above. You count the blooming of the redbuds or the dogwoods in the spring and the changing seasons that follow all too soon. You enjoy as much of it as you can today, and hope, just hope there is a tomorrow.

THE MONEY BAG

I had a customer several years ago who had a thriving convenience market. He sold gas, bait and groceries and he had a large game room. Each night he carried all the money from the store home with him. Sometimes he would have the receipts from two or three days in the bag at one time.

One morning as he started to get in his car, he had the money bag in one hand and a cup of coffee in the other. He laid the money bag on top of the car. He opened the car door and got in, leaving the money bag on top of the car. He said it had about ten thousand dollars in it. He said he never thought about it again until he got to the market. He never saw it again.

THE NEW CADILLAC

This same market was bought later by a man who worked for a big grocery store. His plan was for his wife to manage the market with him helping in his spare time. She did well with it while he kept his job managing the big store.

He did so well managing the big store the man who owned it gave him a new Cadillac as a bonus. He and his wife had both worked hard and had done well so they decided to take the new car and go on a vacation.

They headed out west and during their trip they wound up down in Mexico.

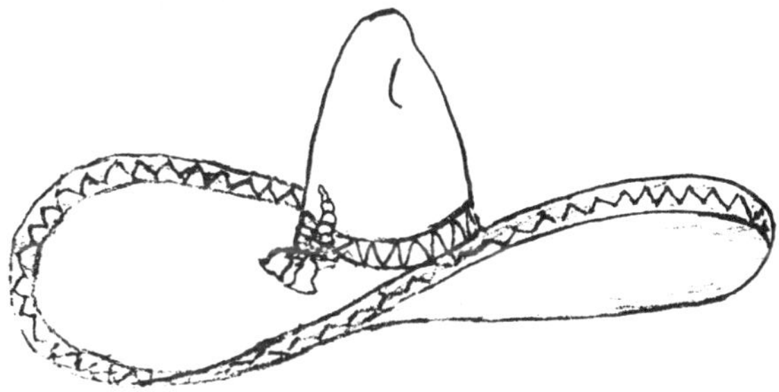

When they crossed the border they had no insurance.

Now everybody who has ever been down there knows there are two things you don't do. You don't drive a good automobile down there and you definitely don't drink their water.

They drive like they are in a

demolition derby. Red lights and stop signs are an absolute waste of the peso. They go through them, blowing their horns and bluffing their way through. Losing a fender here and there doesn't mean a thing to them.

This couple had not been warned about the maniacal habits of these people so they drove their new Cadillac right into the middle of it all. The first day they got their new car totaled. They got a cab back into town and made arrangements to get their car towed back across the border. When they got back to the scene of the accident the next day everything that had not been totaled in the wreck had been stolen. They had stolen the tires, wheels, bumpers, fenders, battery, lights and everything. There wasn't enough left to sell for scrap iron.

THE PET DUCK

All the big commercial docks I have sold bait to over the years have had a goodly number of ducks. While at one of these docks one day I noticed a half grown duck following one of the dock hands around. Everywhere the boy went the duck was right behind.

He was a funny looking duck. He looked like he was crossed up with a woodpecker. You could tell he had been well fed because his body and skin had outgrown his feathers. He just had a feather every now and then.

While I was putting in their bait the boy came up and said, "Let me show you my pet duck." He looked all around the dock to make sure the dock owner was not around, then he picked the duck up and set him over in the cricket box. The duck began eating crickets. I mean he was like a vacuum cleaner. He must have eaten twenty dollars worth of crickets in about two minutes.

I have thought a lot of times since then, if all my customers had a boy and a duck I would have to get a bigger truck.

HIGH PRESSURE SELLING

While driving from stop to stop I have had a lot of time to think and wonder why some shops sell a lot of bait and everything else and some shops don't sell much at all.

I never have thought of myself as a salesman. At all the shops and stores where I go the people know when I walk in what I have. They either want worms or they don't want worms. If they don't,

High Pressure Selling

I get in my truck and go on down the road. It's that simple.

I remember when I had just turned eighteen and had just graduated from high school, I encountered my first high pressure salesmen.

I had walked home from my first job which was about five miles up the road. A car drove into the driveway and two well dressed men got out.

They introduced themselves and told me they wanted to talk about my financial condition. I told them my finances weren't much and I had just started my first job. They were insurance salesmen.

They started telling me since I had turned eighteen and had a paying job I should start being accountable for myself and should not burden my parents with the awful expense of a funeral should I get killed. They assured me they knew how my friends and I drove too fast and how we went down to the river and jumped from the bluff and called ourselves having fun.

They continued reminding me that

these things were dangerous and how awful and downright dishonest it would be if I got killed and incurred the expense of a funeral with no hope of ever paying this debt. The more they talked the worse it got. They were high pressure. They even reminded me of the severity of the wrath of God upon those who did not pay their debts. They scared the daylights out of me. I bought the policy.

This kind of high pressure will not work in selling bait. If people don't want worms you can forget it. Even if it worked, I can't imagine my going out and giving the bait business the bad reputation that insurance salesmen, car salesmen and lawyers have earned for themselves.

WHERE THE EAGLES FLY

I worked a two county area once where I never could sell much. I wore out two trucks before I figured it out. I finally figured out that I was selling all the bait I carried over there during the first ten days of

Where the Eagles Fly

the month. The last two weeks of the month I didn't sell anything

I asked a store owner named Jack, who I had gotten to know well, what was the reason for this unusual pattern. He looked at me kind of funny and said, "We don't sell anything over here except during the first ten days of the month because the eagle flies on the third day of each month."

I still didn't quite understand. I kept running and as I drove I was always looking out the window in search of the eagles. I never saw one. One day I had another talk with Jack. I told him I thought I would have to give up on that part of my route, at least until the eagles could fly more often. I had much more luck selling over where the ducks were.

JACK RETIRES

I was feeling bad about quitting the route, mostly because of Jack. Even though he only bought a little bait the first week of each month he had become a good friend. As it turned out about the time I was quitting the route, Jack told me he was thinking about retiring. He told me he had made a few dollars fixing flats and selling gas and bait. He figured he could rent his building for about three hundred dollars a month and raise a big garden and he could get by pretty good.

He didn't ask my advice and I certainly didn't offer any, but I couldn't see how a forty year old man with a worn out car and a pregnant wife could retire. I guess it seemed like a good idea to him at the time, but it didn't last. His retirement lasted less than a year.

The people who bought his business and rented his building made some changes right away. They busted up his minnow tank and threw it out in the yard and covered up his tire machine with junk. They changed the gas pumps from full service to self service and waited for the cash to flow. It never did. The business fizzled.

Jack took the business back after a few months. In three days he was back in full swing. All he did was put up a sign that read, "FLATS FIXED." Over in that part of the country, if you can fix flats you can get plenty of work. You can't get rich but you surely can get famous. There are people over there who don't know who the governor is, but they know everybody in a two county area who fixes flats.

DIFFERENT STROKES

I think one of the greatest positives of being in the business I am in is the exposure to the many people and their different ideas about doing a job. It has always been interesting to watch the great difference in ways people handle their business. Over the years, I have seen business swap from one side of the road to the other, and then back again. I have seen good businesses ruined through mis-management and some lost purely to bad luck or fire. I have seen some succeed by hard work and others lost after years of hard work and sacrifice when the skills to hold it together were just not there.

COUNTRY FOLKS

Another enjoyable part of the business has been the traveling of roads that reach into the most remote parts of our area. I have always been fascinated by the people that live and travel on the by-ways and back roads. It seems the more remote an area, the friendlier are it's people.

I have had many people who would wave from their gardens or from their front porches as I passed. I have watched some for several years, never knowing their names, yet waving to them many times as I traveled their roads two or three times a week. I have watched as some grew older and their lives diminished till waving at passersby seemed to be the highlight of their day. I have watched as fall and winter came and they retreated back into the warmth of their homes. I have felt sadness when some did not re-appear the next summer.

ABOUT DEATH AND DYING

As I have driven into some area I have always noticed with great interest, the well kept cemeteries along the way. Many are small plots with only a few graves while some are larger. Many of the smaller plots have an ornate fence around the boundary and some have an archway at the entrance. The one thing that seems to be common to all, they are neatly trimmed and manicured.

I have always assumed this was a combined effort by family, friends and neighbors in these country communities. It is an expression of their love for their family and friends and a testament of their respect for the dead.

These people hold fast to traditions such as pulling to the side of the road as an oncoming hearse approaches. There are no exceptions.

One day as I drove along a country road which leads down to a boat dock where I delivered, I noticed over on a shaded hillside there was one of these cemeteries. The road leading to the cemetery went up the hill and then made a complete circle around the top of the small knoll. Inside the circle next to a new grave, there stood an old man. His hair shined in the sun and was as white as snow. Just below the grave on the road there was parked, a little tan car.

As I drove on, I thought about the old man and guessed he had probably lost his wife, however I had no way of knowing. As the weeks and months passed, I continued to make deliveries down the road. It didn't matter which day of the week or what time of day I went by, the little tan car and the old man were over on the hill. Some days he would be standing, with his arms folded, his back stooped from age, some days he would be sitting on a nearby stump. Always his hair shined as white as snow.

I had told my wife, Betty, about seeing the old man for well over a year. One day she rode with me on this route so I anticipated showing her as we drove down the dead end road to the dock. As we came upon the cemetery, much to my surprise, the tan car and the old man were not there. We drove on down the road and I put in some bait at the dock, which took about thirty minutes. I kept wondering about the old man. This was the first time I had come by when he was not there. After we left the dock, we went back up the road by the cemetery and there on the hill was the little car and the old man. I have seen him many times since then. To some of us who have never walked in the old man's shoes this may seem strange but each of us has a unique and different way to show respect or to grieve or to remember.

When I was very young, I had an uncle who died. He was only twenty seven years old. I remember when he died, I could not understand why people came to my grandmother's house with fried chicken, cakes and pies. I was young, naive and unknowing, but I could not relate the death of my uncle to all the food, the cakes and pies. I didn't understand that these things were being brought by some of the best people on earth. They were friends, they were neighbors and they were people who cared and were doing what they could to comfort and help during a bad time.

I didn't understand. I knew I was not hungry, so I didn't eat their chicken or their pies. I knew I had lost the uncle with whom I shared the same middle name and I knew I was feeling a hurt that was coming from deep inside which I had never felt before. I knew he was who I thought about at night till I went to sleep. He was the first thing I thought about when I awoke. I kept remembering the times not too long before when he pulled me in my wagon. I remembered the times when he sat me on his knee. I remembered the times when he would peel an apple with his pocket knife, always giving me the first slice. This was my first experience with death and I remember well, it was not easy.

Many years later my daddy passed

away. There had been a noticeable difference in customs during this thirty two years. The bringing of food will always be an admirable and helpful show of love and compassion. The donation of money to charity and the donation of books and bibles in memory of the deceased was more widely practiced. The sending of flowers was more prevalent. I had never seen more flowers at a funeral before.

Daddy lived about fifteen miles from his bait shop. His funeral was held at a funeral home not far from where he lived. His bait shop was fifteen miles away.

During the early years of building and running his bait shop he had become friends with several of the kids who lived nearby. He let them trade empty coke bottles for cokes and candy, sometimes he hired them to sweep the floor for enough money to buy treats. His relationship with each kid was different. To all he was a friend.

He lay at the funeral home on a cold January night. It was bitter cold with a snow on the ground that had lingered for days. A kid known as "Peanut" came into the funeral parlor. "Peanut" signed the register and then stood and talked with us for a while. During the conversation, I realized "Peanut" was alone and I knew he was in his early teens and not old enough to drive. I asked him how he had gotten there. He said, "I walked." Realizing the night was bitter cold, I offered to take him back home. His answer, I will never forget. He said he had walked the fifteen miles down and he wanted to walk back. He said as he walked, he had remembered the good times he had enjoyed and shared with daddy as he was growing up. He remembered the cokes, the candy, the laughs and the times he had sold crawfish and coke bottles for cash. He remembered their friendship while he walked and how much their friendship had meant to him. He said the walk was for "Mr. Jim" and even if it had been fifty miles he would have gladly walked it "for him."

"TWINK"

During the years of working the bait business, especially the retail business, we formed many friendships with people who liked to fish. They were old and young, rich and poor and from every walk of life. Many we only got to know and see as they came through the shop in a hurry to get bait, on their way to the lake. Many we got to know and formed friendships that would last a lifetime.

One of the lasting friendships was formed with a boy named "Twink." "Twink" liked fishing better than any one I have ever known. He could reach a level of excitement over a fishing trip that was almost unreal. He knew what it took to catch fish. The biggest string of fish my son, "Buddy," ever caught, he caught it with "Twink." The biggest string of fish my son, Charlie, ever caught, he caught it with "Twink." The biggest string of fish I ever caught, I caught it with "Twink."

Throughout his life he was addicted to alcohol. He would readily admit he had a problem which he fought every day. He lived his life, one day at a time. Each day he could live through without drinking was an accomplishment.

When we didn't see him for several days we became concerned, because we knew he was hid out somewhere, drinking. When Betty's mother passed away, we had not seen "Twink" for several days. The first night at the funeral home, Betty and I were standing in a crowd near the casket. We looked across the room toward the front door as "Twink" walked in. We said to each other at once, "There's "Twink".

He stood as his eyes searched the entire crowd. When he saw us, he came as straight as an arrow, across the room. He was as sober as could be. He had stayed sober this day for us.

He was visibly nervous, uncomfortable and upset. He stood as he tried to gain his composure with tears in his eyes. Then he said in his usual slow, southern drawl, "I don't know what I'm s'posed to say, but all's I know is I really do love y'all and I felt

My Friend, "TWINK"

like I wanted to come".

"Twink" may not have known, but he had said it all. What he had said had come from his heart. He reaffirmed and reassured me of what I already knew, he was my friend.

"Twink" continued fishing and continued his battle against alcoholism over the next few years. He lost the battle in the spring of 1998 at the age of forty. He was the third of four siblings to lose this battle. Helping "Twink's" mother and daddy to say good-bye was one of the hardest things my family and I have had to do in a long time. We miss him a lot.

OTHER DELIVERY PEOPLE

Also, I have made some lasting friendships with other delivery people I have gotten to know. Most of them I never knew their names, so I tagged them with a nick-name as most of them did to me. I became "Bait Man," "Worm man," "Minnow Man," or "Cricket" or just plain "Bait". Occasionally, I get called "Wormy." That's all right, because it's all in fun.

I have known several "Bread Men" and "Mail Men." One "Mail Man" I remember in particular was always a jovial and friendly sort of guy. He always wanted me to carry the mail along with the bait. He figured since we both ran about the same roads, I could do the mail and the bait and he could go fishing. He was real truthful about it too. He said I didn't even have to know how to read. He said you just leave a piece or two in every box and make sure you don't have any left over at the end of the day. That's all there is to it.

I always wanted to try it but he

retired before I got a chance. About a month before he retired he put a big sign in the rear window of his car which counted down the days until his retirement. I miss him a lot.

I knew a produce man who I called "Cabbage." His truck had a sign on it that said "Produce" but mostly all I ever saw him have was cabbage.

MILK MAN

"Milk Man" has been a good friend for a long time. One fall day several years ago we were in a bait shop making deliveries. As usual, we were talking and passing time and the subject of ginseng came up. "Milk Man" said he had dug a lot of ginseng roots and that they brought several hundred dollars a pound. I knew this because I had two or three customers who dug, but I had never seen any growing in the woods. As we talked on he told me he would show me what it looked like some time. The store owner told us there was some growing out the ridge behind his shop. We decided to leave our trucks parked at the bait shop and back through the woods we went, hunting ginseng. It has five leaves on a stem and has scarlet berries. It grows only a few inches tall. From that day on "Milk Man" became "Ginseng."

LITTLE BOY BLUE

I saw "Little Boy Blue" only once but I'll never forget him. One day as I started to enter an old, country store there was a young guy coming out. As he started across the small parking lot to his log truck, a man leaning against the front of the old store said, "Little Boy Blue, blow your horn." I stepped inside the store, closing the screened door behind me. As the log truck rolled in front of the store, "Little Boy Blue" blew his horn. It was a train horn mounted on the log truck. I mean it was forever more LOUD. The bags of potato chips laying on the rack just inside the store were bouncing up and down. I wanted to run, but I didn't know which way. I couldn't imagine what was

Little Boy Blue

happening. I had heard about women that were ugly enough to make a freight train turn down a dirt road. I had seen two or three up there that were at least that ugly, if not uglier. I was afraid that was what was happening. It sounded like a train was coming right through the store.

After it was over and I had figured out what had happened, it really was funny. I have looked for the truck since but I have never seen it again.

IT'S BEEN GREAT FUN

As I think back over the many miles I have driven, the many friends I have made, and the good times I have had, I can truly say if I had it to do over, I would do it all again. Life as well as business has it's ups and downs. My ups have far outweighed the downs. The highs have always outnumbered the lows. The difference has been in the many friends and the many good customers I have had. Their loyalty and their friendship and their down to earth nature has inspired me to keep on keeping on.

So, for as long as I am able, I guess I will load my truck with bait and head down the road to see what I might find.

Who knows, there may be another little man, like Mr. Myers, stooped by his many years of hard work and selling bait, realizing his life is about over, look at me and say "Good-bye, Honey, I wish you well." There may be a lovely little lady like Mrs. Red, ask me in to "try" some of her peach pie.

Or if I'm lucky, maybe, just maybe, there will be another little girl like Susie or Missy who will make me her "Daddy Number Two" and give a lifetime of unconditional friendship and love.